⌣	close up space
℘	delete
℘	delete and close up space
#	separate with a space
∧	insert here what is indicated in the margin
¶	start new paragraph
no ¶	no paragraph; run in with previous paragraph
⊙/	insert period
∧/	insert comma
⌃₃/	insert semicolon
⊙/	insert colon
¹⁄ₘ /	insert em dash
¹⁄ₘ / ¹⁄ₘ	insert pair of em dashes
=/	insert hyphen
ᵛ/	insert apostrophe
cap	use capital letter here
lc	use lowercase letter here
ital	set in italic type
rom	set in roman type
sc	set in small capitals
bf	set in boldface type
tr	transpose letters or words

This book is dedicated to all my students over the years, whose written prose sometimes mystified me, often enlightened me, and invariably beguiled me. Bless them all.

The Little English Handbook: Choices and Conventions

Edward P. J. Corbett
The Ohio State University

John Wiley & Sons, Inc.
New York / London / Sydney / Toronto

Library of Congress Cataloging in Publication Data:

Corbett, Edward P   J
  The little English handbook.

  1. English language—Rhetoric. I. Title.

PE1408.C587   808'.042   72-11761
ISBN 0-471-17230-8

Printed in the United States of America

10 9 8 7

Preface

This handbook is designed to serve as a guide on basic matters of grammar, style, paragraphing, punctuation, and mechanics for those engaged in writing public prose. By ''public prose'' is meant that dialect of written English most commonly used in the newspapers, magazines, and books that the majority of educated native speakers read. This ranges in style from the formal to the casual, from the literary to the colloquial. But because public prose seeks to be intelligible to a general audience, it avoids the strictly in-group vocabulary of various professional, regional, and social groups, and it observes the rules of grammar as taught in the schools.

The use of this term is not intended to disparage the other current dialects, most of which serve well the needs of some of the people all of the time and all of the people some of the time. Obviously, spoken English, with its own wide range of professional, regional, and social dialects, serves the needs of more people more often than written English does. In fact, many people speak more words in a single week than they will write during a lifetime. When linguists say that the spoken language is the primary language, they mean that the spoken comes first in point of time (centuries before the written form developed) and use (in a single lifetime, before the written language is learned). Also, more natives have a command

Preface

of the spoken language than have a command of both the spoken and the written. However, despite the primacy of the spoken language, there are occasions when many, if not most, native speakers must use the written language in order to record or communicate their thoughts, needs, and feelings. It is for those occasions that this handbook is designed.

When a person wishes to communicate in the written medium, it is natural for him to resort—or wish that he could resort—to a more sophisticated style of language than the one he is accustomed to use in the conduct of his everyday affairs. Actually, in his first fumbling efforts at writing, he might succeed better if he used the lexical and syntactical resources acquired from daily practice in the oral medium. But as the written transcription of impromptu talk reveals, the spoken language is often marked by redundancy of language, imprecision of diction, and loose, rambling, dislocated sentence patterns. Words and structures that may have communicated adequately in the oral medium because of the aid furnished by voice and gesture are something less than adequate when inscribed on paper. For effective written communication, words must be more precise, structures tighter, and organization more discernible; and graphic devices of punctuation and mechanics must be relied on to do what the intonation of the voice does in the oral medium. The kind of public prose used by newscasters on television and radio and by writers in newspapers, magazines, and books has proven to be the most efficient medium for communicating on paper with a general audience.

In this little handbook, I concentrate on those matters of grammar, style, paragraphing, punctuation, and mechanics that from years of experience in reading student papers and responding to telephone queries from businessmen and secretaries I know to be the most common and persistent problems in the expressive part of the writing process. For answers to the larger or more subtle problems in writing prose, you will have to consult one of the comprehensive rhetoric handbooks that are readily available. I do not, for instance, provide guidance in all the uses of the comma; some of these are never or seldom a problem for writers. Instead, I deal only with those half-dozen conventions of the comma that are most often ignored or abused and that are most crucial for the preservation of clarity. If you master these six, you can rest assured that there are no really serious mistakes that you can make in the use (or omission) of the comma.

Nor does this handbook carry a section that is a common feature of comprehensive handbooks, the glossary of usage. Although questions of usage—whether to use *contact* as a verb, the conjunction *like* or *as*, the preposition *due to* or *because of*, the construction *different than* or *different from*—are troublesome problems, a glossary of usage has been excluded from this handbook for two reasons: (1) to be really useful, it would have to be at least thirty pages long, which would make this a bigger book than I wanted, and (2) even if I knew more than I do about the current status of certain locutions, I would find it difficult to make pronouncements about questions of usage outside the norm of a context. If the writer has a question about usage, he can consult one of the book-length authorities, such as H. W. Fowler's *A Dictionary of Modern English Usage*, Bergen and Cornelia Evans's *A Dictionary of Contemporary American Usage*, or Wilson Follett's *Modern American Usage*.

The subtitle of this handbook, *Choices and Conventions*, reflects my approach to the matters I deal with. Some of the principles governing the system of writing have been established by convention; others represent a recommendation from a number of available options. Accordingly, in most cases, I have stated the guiding principle in definite, unequivocal

Preface

terms. It should quickly be added, however, that there are no absolute prescriptions in matters of language. Where choices are available, a selection must be guided by a consideration of the subject matter, occasion, desired effect, and audience. But in my experience, the kind of person who needs the guidance of a handbook like this wants a simple, straightforward answer to his query—e.g. "How do I punctuate this compound sentence?" He does not yet have enough sophistication in the use of the written language to be much helped by the advice, "In most cases, you should separate the two clauses of a compound sentence with a comma, but often when the clauses are short, you can dispense with the comma without any loss of clarity." Such a person is better served if he is told that he should *always* put a comma in front of the coordinating conjunction that joins the two independent clauses of a compound sentence. There is also a practical value attaching to the unequivocal advice: rarely will the writer go wrong if he follows it, but he may expect to go wrong on occasion if he ignores it.

It is assumed that the user of this handbook has acquired at least a basic knowledge of formal grammar and that the grammatical system to which he has most likely been exposed is the "traditional" one. Thus when such terms as *compound sentence, independent clause, participial phrase* are used, the writer will probably be able to recognize the structures to which the terms refer. Also, the diagram of structures that accompanies many of the statements of principle will serve as a visual aid for those whose knowledge of traditional terminology has faded and for those whose training has been predominantly in structural grammar or in transformational-generative grammar. Thus, the "picture" of a structure will usually be a sufficient guide for those who are impatient with, or are baffled by, technical terminology. However, to ensure maximum comprehension, I have furnished the book with a glossary of grammatical terms.

About 90 percent of the examples—both those that illustrate the observance of the principle and those that illustrate the violation of it—have been taken directly from student writing. A few examples had to be invented, but even these are typical of sentences that students write. In the case of those examples that illustrate violations of the principle, no ridicule of the writer is intended. I simply want to exhibit, from prose written in the 1970s, examples of aberrations from the prevailing conventions. In the explanatory matter that follows the examples, I frequently show why the aberration is a threat to clear communication and how it might be corrected.

By concentrating on matters of grammar, style, paragraphing, punctuation, and mechanics, I do not wish to imply that these are the most important concerns of "good writing." What is most essential for effective communication is the substance, originality, and sophistication of one's thoughts and the ability to organize them in a unified, coherent way. However, sloppy articulation of one's thoughts is often a reflection of sloppy inventional and organizational processes; it is easily demonstrable that careless expression stems ultimately from careless thinking. Observance of the "basics" treated in this handbook will not guarantee that your prose will be interesting or worth reading, but observance of the fundamental conventions of the writing system will at least guarantee that your prose *can* be read. Readable prose is no mean achievement. The next achievement to strive for is to write prose that others will *want* to read.

Edward P. J. Corbett

Note to the Writer

You are fortunate if you have an instructor or an editor or a knowledgeable friend who will read what you have written and call attention to the strengths and weaknesses of your prose by writing comments in the margin or at the end of your paper. Comments of that sort, especially when they are judicious and constructive, can be of great help to you in improving your writing. You should value those personal notes, and whenever the correction, question, suggestion, praise, or blame in them strikes you as being well grounded, you would do well to heed it.

To call attention, however, to routine matters of grammar, style, paragraphing, punctuation, or mechanics, your accommodating critic may resort to some kind of shorthand notations. If he knows that you have a copy of this handbook, he may underline or encircle something in your manuscript and write a number in the margin. If, for instance, he scribbles the number 83 in the margin, he is suggesting that you look at item 83 in the section on mechanics. Turning to this item in the handbook, you will find that it has to do with italicizing certain kinds of titles. Perhaps you failed to italicize the title of a book you mentioned, or perhaps instead of italicizing the title of the book, you enclosed it in quotation marks. The principle stated opposite the number 83 may be all that you need to read. But if you need further enlightenment about what you have done wrong, you can look at the graphic diagram of the structure involved (if one is presented for that principle) or at the examples printed below the principle, or you can go on to read the explanation of the principle.

For more complicated matters, the explanation in the handbook may not be sufficient to point out what you have done wrong or to prevent you from making the mistake again. If so, you should arrange to have a conference with the critic of your prose. Although the correction symbols in the margin may strike you as being heartlessly impersonal, it would be a mistake for you to regard them as petulant slaps on the wrist. They are intended to help you discover how to put your written prose in the "proper" form.

This handbook is also intended to serve as a guide to the writer who does not have an instructor or a friend to read and criticize what he has written. Usually, once a writer has completed a freshman English course or an advanced composition course of some kind, he no longer enjoys the advantage of frequent, expert criticism of his prose. (If he does, he probably has to pay for the service.) If kept at hand, along with such other reference books as a dictionary and a thesaurus, this handbook can be a useful guide for the writer when he sits down to write something that he wants others to read. The reference charts on the endpages will direct him to the section that deals with his particular problem of the moment. For example, "Should the modifying clause in this sentence be enclosed with commas?" Somewhere in its pages, the handbook probably provides a straightforward answer to that query.

Acknowledgments

Every textbook designed for the classroom profits from the criticisms and suggestions of experienced, knowledgeable teachers. I have been especially fortunate in the reviewers who have criticized my manuscript in its various stages: James T. Nardin of Louisiana State University, Gary Tate of Texas Christian University, William F. Irmscher of the University of Washington, James Karabatsos of Creighton University, Marinus Swets of Grand Rapids Junior College, Richard Lloyd-Jones of the University of Iowa, Mina P. Shaughnessy of City College of the City University of New York, Kirby L. Duncan of Stephen F. Austin University, Nancy Dasher of Ohio State University, Betty Renshaw of Prince George's Community College, and Raymond D. Liedlich of Portland Community College. I have also benefited from the judicious advice and careful editing of the staff of John Wiley, especially Thomas O. Gay and Arthur Vergara. I am indebted also to those standard handbooks and meticulously edited magazines that have instructed me all these years about the choices and conventions of written English. The errors and shortcomings of the book should be attributed solely to me.

E. P. J. C.

Contents

Contents

Contents

Mechanics   80–89

Format of Research Paper

Contents

Forms for Letters

Legend

Some of the principles, especially those having to do with punctuation, are illustrated with graphic models, using these symbols:

$$\boxed{} = \text{word}$$

A word inside the box designates a particular part of speech, e.g. $\boxed{\text{noun}}$.

_____ = phrase.

The following abbreviations on the horizontal line designate a particular kind of phrase, e.g.$\underline{\text{prep.}}$:

prep. = prepositional phrase (**on the stagecoach**).
part. = participial phrase (**having ridden on the stage-coach**).
ger. = gerund phrase (**riding on the stagecoach** pleased him).
inf. = infinitive phrase (he wanted **to ride on the stage-coach**).

Legend

 = independent clause

An independent clause, sometimes referred to as a "main clause," can stand by itself as a grammatically complete sentence, e.g. **He rode on the stagecoach.**

 = dependent clause

A dependent clause cannot stand by itself as a grammatically complete sentence. The following abbreviations printed above the first vertical line designate a particular kind of dependent clause, e.g. noun.

noun = noun clause (He claimed **that he rode on the stagecoach**).

adj. = adjective clause (The man **who rode on the stagecoach** was pleased).

adv. = adverb clause (He was late **because he rode on the stagecoach**).

Format of Manuscript

In preparing the final draft of a manuscript, follow the specific directions about format given by your instructor or editor. However, if no specific directions are given, you can be confident that the format of your manuscript will be acceptable if you observe the following conventions:

11

Write on one side of the paper only.

12

Double-space the lines of prose, whether you handwrite or typewrite.

A manuscript submitted to an editor for consideration must be typewritten and double-spaced.

13

Preserve a left-hand and a right-hand margin.

On the left-hand side leave at least a $1\frac{1}{2}$-inch margin. On the right-hand side try to preserve about a 1-inch margin. If you are handwriting your manuscript on theme paper, the vertical red line will set your left-hand margin.

Format of Manuscript

14

Put the title of your paper at the top of the first page of your manuscript—even though you may have put the title on a cover sheet.

See **84** for instructions about how to set down the title of your paper.

15

Number all pages, after the first one, at the top of the page, in the middle or at the right-hand margin.

Be sure to assemble the pages of your manuscript in the right sequence.

16

Secure your manuscript with a paper clip— *never* with a staple or pin.

Many editors will not even read a manuscript that is stapled together.

17

Use the proper kind of paper.

If you typewrite your manuscript, use white, unlined paper. If you handwrite your manuscript, use white, lined theme paper. Never submit a formal written assignment on pages torn from a spiral notebook.

Grammar

Grammar may be defined as the study of how a language "works"—a study of how the structural system of a language combines with a vocabulary to convey meaning. When we study a foreign language in school, we must study both **vocabulary** and **grammar,** and until we can put the two together, we cannot translate the language. Sometimes we know the meaning of every word in a foreign-language sentence, and yet we cannot translate the sentence because we cannot figure out its grammar. On the other hand, we sometimes can figure out the syntax of the foreign-language sentence, but because we do not know the meaning of one or more words in the sentence, we still cannot translate the sentence.

If a native speaker of English heard or read this sequence of words

> The porturbs in the brigger torms have tanted the makrets' rotment brokly.

he would perceive that the sequence bears a marked resemblance to an English sentence. Although many words in that sequence would be unfamiliar to him, he would detect that the sequence had the structure of the kind of English sentence that makes a statement, and he might further surmise that this kind of statement pattern was one that said that *porturbs* (whoever they are) had done something to *rotment* (whatever that is) or, to put it another way, that *porturbs* is the subject

Grammar

of the sentence, that *have tanted* is the predicate verb (transitive), and that *rotment* is the object of that transitive verb, the receiver of the action performed by the doer, *porturbs*. How was he able to make that much "sense" out of that sequence of strange words? He was able to detect that much "sense" by noting the following structural signals:

☐ **Function words:**

The three occurrences of the article **the;** the preposition **in;** and the auxiliary verb **have.**

☐ **Inflections and affixes:**

The **-s** added to nouns to form the plural; the **-er** added to adjectives to form the comparative degree; the **-ed** added to verbs to form the past tense or the past participle; the **-s'** added to nouns to form the plural possessive case; the affix **-ment** added to certain words to form an abstract noun; and the **-ly** added to adjectives to form adverbs.

☐ **Word order.**

The basic pattern of a statement or declarative sentence in English is S (subject) + V (verb) + C (complement) or NP (noun phrase) + VP (verb phrase). In the sequence, **The porturbs in the brigger torms** appears to be the S or NP part of the sentence and **have tanted the makrets' rotment brokly** the VP part of the sentence (**have tanted** being the V and **the makrets' rotment brokly** being the C).

(a) **Intonation (stress, pitch, terminals, and juncture).** If the sequence were spoken aloud, the native speaker would detect that the sequence had the intonational pattern of a declarative sentence in spoken English.

(b) **Punctuation and mechanics.** If the sequence were written out (as it is here), the native speaker would observe that the sequence began with a capital letter and ended with a period, two typographical devices that signal a statement sentence in written English.

The native speaker of English has been able to read all of this meaning into the string of nonsense words simply by observing the *grammatical* devices of **inflections, function words, word order,** and **intonation** (if spoken) or **punctuation** (if written). Now, if he had a dictionary that defined such words as *porturb, brig, torm, tant, makret, rotment,* and *brok,* he would be able to translate the full meaning of the sentence. But by observing the structural or grammatical devices alone, the native speaker of English has perceived that the sequence of words

> The porturbs in the brigger torms have tanted the makrets' rotment brokly.

exactly matches the structure of an English sentence like this one:

> The citizens in the larger towns have accepted the legislators' commitment enthusiastically.

What he has been concentrating on is the *grammar* of the sentence, and it is in this sense that we use the term *grammar* in the section that follows.

Almost every child has mastered the fundamentals of this grammatical system of English by the time he starts school. He has "mastered grammar" in the sense that he can form original and meaningful English sentences of his own and can understand English sentences uttered by others. He may not "know grammar" in the sense that he can analyze the structure of sentences and label the parts, but he knows grammar in the sense that he can *perform appropriately* in the language—that is, that he can utter and respond to properly formed sentences.

In a sense, the grammar of a language is a convention.

5

Grammar

We formulate sentences in a certain way because communities of native speakers of the language, over a long period of time, have developed, and agreed on, certain ways of saying something. The grammar of a language allows some choices but proscribes others. For instance, if you wanted to tell someone that a certain boy kissed a certain girl in a certain manner, grammar would allow you one of these choices of patterns:

> The boy kissed the girl passionately.
> The boy passionately kissed the girl.
> Passionately the boy kissed the girl.
> The girl was kissed passionately by the boy.

Grammar would not allow you to use one of these patterns:

> The girl kissed the boy passionately.

> (this is a grammatical sentence, but because of the altered word order, it does not say what you wanted to say. Here the girl is the doer of the action, and the boy is the receiver of the action)

> The passionately boy the girl kissed.

> Kissed boy the passionately girl the.

The choice of which grammatically acceptable pattern a writer will use is a concern of style, which will be dealt with in the next section.

In this section on grammar, we are dealing with those devices of *inflection, function words,* and *word order* that must be observed if written sentences are to convey the intended meaning to a reader clearly and unequivocally. We do not deal in this section with *intonation,* because this handbook is concerned only with the written language. In a later section of this handbook, we shall deal with the fourth grammatical device of written English, *punctuation.*

20

Use an apostrophe for the possessive, or genitive, case of the noun.

Here are some guidelines on forming the possessive, or genitive, case of the English noun:

(a) As indicated in the diagrams above, most English nouns form the possessive case with 's (singular) or s' (plural). (An alternative form of the genitive consists of an **of** phrase: **the general's commands** or **the commands of the general**).

(b) The possessive case of nouns that form their plural in ways other than by adding an **s** is formed by adding 's to the plural of the noun: **man's/men's, woman's/women's, child/children's, ox's/oxen's, deer's/deer's, mouse's/mice's.**

(c) Some writers simply add an apostrophe to form the possessive case of nouns ending in **s**:

the actress' fame

the alumnus' contribution

Keats' odes

Dickens' death

However, other writers add the usual 's to form the possessive case of such nouns: **actress's, alumnus's** (plural, **alumni's**), **Keats's, Dickens's.** Take your choice, but be consistent.

(d) The rules for forming the possessive case of pairs of

Grammar

nouns are as follows: (1) in the case of joint possession, add 's only to the second member of the pair: **John and Mary's mother, the brother and sister's car,** and (2) in the case of individual possession, add 's to each member of the pair: **the boy's and girl's bedroom, John's and Mary's tennis rackets, the men's and women's locker rooms.**

(e) Form the possessive case of group nouns and compound nouns by adding 's to the end of the unit: **commander in chief's, someone else's, president-elect's, editor in chief's, son-in-law's.** In the case of those compounds that form their plural by adding **s** to the first word, form the plural possessive case by adding 's to the end of the unit: **editors in chief's, sons-in-law's.**

(f) Normally the 's or s' is reserved for the genitive case of nouns naming animate creatures (human beings and animals). The **of** phrase is commonly used for the genitive case of inanimate nouns: not **the house's roof** but **the roof of the house.** Usage, however, sanctions the use of 's with a few inanimate nouns: **a day's wages, a week's work, the year's death toll, the school's policies.**

21

Its is the possessive case of the pronoun it; it's is the contraction of it is or it has.

More mistakes have been made with the pronoun **it** than with any other single word in the English language. The mistakes result from confusion about the two **s** forms of this pronoun. **It's** is used where **its** is the correct form (**The dog broke it's leg** instead of **The dog broke its leg**), and **its** is used where **it's** is the correct form (**Its a shame that the girl broke her leg** instead of **It's a shame that the girl broke her leg**).

The writer who uses **it's** for the possessive case of **it** is probably influenced by the **'s** that is used to form the possessive case of the singular noun (**man's hat**). He might be helped to avoid this mistake if he would remember that none of the personal pronouns uses **'s** to form its possessive case: **I/my, you/your, he/his, she/her, it/its, we/our, they/their.** So he should write, **The company lost its lease.**

Or the writer might be helped to avoid this mistake if he would remember that the apostrophe has another function in written English: to indicate the omission of one or more letters in an English word, as in contractions (**I'll, don't, he'd**). The apostrophe in the word **it's** signals the contraction of the expression **it is** or **it has.** So he should write, **It's the first loss the company has suffered** or **It's come to my attention that you are frequently late.**

Don't let this little word defeat you. Get **it** right, once and for all.

22

The predicate verb should agree in number with its subject.

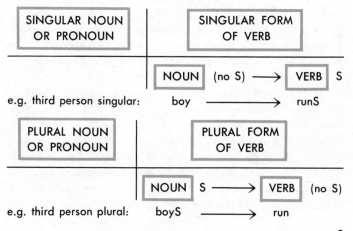

Grammar

In addition to these differentiated forms of the verb in the third person, present tense, we have to be concerned about the few differentiated forms of the verb **to be (am/is/are; was/were)** and of auxiliary verbs **(has/have; does/do)**.

The English verb has been evolving toward a single form for the singular and plural of all three persons (first, second, third)—as witness the **-ed** ending added to the verb in all three persons, singular and plural, of the past tense—and we may yet live to see the day when a totally simplified form of the English verb is achieved. In the meanwhile, the few remaining differentiated forms of the verb will probably continue to give writers some trouble.

Some typical examples of faulty agreement:

1 He **don't** care about anything.
2 The lawyer and his client **agrees** on a fee.
3 If any one of the substations **are knocked** out, we can resort to reserve stations.
4 The jury **has** made up **their** minds.

Expressions like **He don't care about anything** are not so much "mistakes" in agreement as carry-overs from the dialect that a person speaks, quite acceptably, in his community. Such a person should be made aware of the standard form of the verb in written prose: **He doesn't care about anything** (a singular verb with a singular subject).

Most errors of agreement in written prose are the result of carelessness, inadvertence, or uncertainty. The writer often knows better; he merely slips up. Errors in agreement often occur when several words intervene between the simple subject of the sentence and the predicate verb, as in our third example above: **If any one of the substations are knocked out.** . . . The simple subject of the **if** clause here is **one,** but because the plural noun **substations** (the object of the preposition **of**) intervened between that singular subject and the verb, the writer was influenced to use the plural form of the verb (**are knocked out**) instead of the correct singular form (**is knocked out**). Careful proofreading will often catch such inadvertent errors of agreement.

Errors due to uncertainty are another matter. Uncertainty about whether the verb should be singular or plural arises in cases where (1) the subject is compound; (2) the subject is a collective noun; (3) the subject of the sentence follows the expletive structure **there is** or **there are**; and (4) the subject takes the form of structures like **one of those who** and **this man as well as.** Here are some guidelines for these puzzling cases:

(a) Compound subject

(1) Singular subjects joined by **and** usually take a plural verb.

John and his sister **were questioned** by the police.

(2) Singular subjects joined by **or** or by the correlative conjunctions **either . . . or, neither . . . nor** take a singular verb.

John or his sister **runs** the store during the week.

Neither John nor his sister **is suspected** of pilfering money from the cash register.

(3) When both subjects are plural, the verb is plural.

The detectives and the insurance agents **have expressed** their belief in the innocence of the brother and sister.

Neither the detectives nor the insurance agents **have expressed** any doubts about the innocence of the brother and sister.

(4) When one subject is singular and the other subject is plural and the subjects are joined by **or** or by the correlative conjunctions **either . . . or, neither . . . nor,**

both . . . and, not only . . . but also, the verb agrees in number with the closest subject.

> Either John or his parents **have agreed** to cooperate with the police.

> Neither the brothers nor the sister **appears** to be cooperative.

(b) Collective noun as subject

(1) If the collective noun is considered as a **group,** the verb is singular.

> The jury **has made up** its mind.

> The committee **was elected** unanimously.

> The number of students drafted last month **was increased** by 50 percent.

(2) If the collective noun is considered as **individuals** of a group, each acting on his own, the verb is plural.

> The jury **have made up** their minds.

> The committee **wish** to offer their congratulations to the new chairman.

> A number of students **have petitioned** the draft board for a deferment.

(c) Expletive structure **there is/was, there was/were**

(1) If the delayed or real subject following the expletive **there** is singular, the verb is singular.

> There **is** a remarkable consensus among the committee members.

(2) If the delayed or real subject following the expletive **there** is plural, the verb is plural.

> There **were** ten dissenting votes from the stockholders.

(d) Special structures

(1) In the structure **one of the** (plural noun) **who,** the predicate verb of the **who** clause is plural, because the antecedent of the subject **who** is the plural noun rather than the singular **one.**

> Matilda is one of the women who **refuse** to accept the ruling.

> (*here the antecedent of* **who** *is the plural noun* **women**)

(2) Exception: if **the only** precedes **one of the** (plural noun) **who,** the predicate verb of the **who** clause is singular, because the subject **who** in that case refers to the singular **one** rather than to the plural object of the preposition **of.**

> Matilda is the only one of the women who **refuses** to accept the ruling.

(3) A singular subject followed by structures like **as well as, in addition to, together with** takes a singular verb.

(A plural subject, of course, followed by any of these structures, would take a plural verb. See the third example below.)

> The sergeant as well as his superior officers **praises** his platoon.

> Gill Dougal along with his roommate **has denied** the charges.

> The students together with their counselor **deny** that there has been any distribution of marijuana in the dorms.

23

A pronoun must agree in person, number, and gender with its antecedent noun.

Grammar

Examples of faulty agreement between a pronoun and its antecedent:

1 A **family** cannot go camping these days without a truckload of gadgets to make **your** campsite look just like home.

2 Each **candidate** was allowed to voice **their** opinion on the subject being discussed.

3 The **university** did not live up to **his** promise to the students.

Pronouns, which are substitutes for nouns, have, in common with nouns, **number** (singular and plural) and **gender** (masculine, feminine, and neuter). What nouns and pronouns do not share in common is the full range of **person.** All nouns are **third person** exclusively; but some pronouns are **first person (I, we),** some are **second person (you),** and some are **third person (e.g. he, she, it, they, one, some, none, all).**

A firm grammatical principle is that a pronoun must correspond with whatever of those three aspects of person, number, and gender it shares with its antecedent noun. A second-person pronoun cannot be linked with a third-person noun (see the first example above); a plural pronoun cannot be linked with a singular noun (see the second example above); a masculine pronoun cannot be linked with a neuter noun (see the third example above).

Simple as the grammatical principle is that governs the relationship of a pronoun with its antecedent, there are a few tricky problems for the writer in making a pronoun agree in person, number, and gender with its noun. For one thing, the English language has no convenient pronoun for indicating masculine-or-feminine gender. When a noun could be either masculine or feminine, a writer is tempted to use an awkward pronoun form like **his or her, his/her,** or **his (her),** as in the following sentence: "The student should bring **his or her** schedule cards to the bursar's office." One way around that awkward locution is to use a plural noun: "**Students** should bring **their** schedule cards to the bursar's office." Another way is to settle for one gender in the pronoun, with the implication that the other sex is included in the reference if applicable: "The student should bring **his** schedule cards to the bursar's office."

Another problem stems from the ambiguity of **number** of such pronouns as **everyone, everybody, all, none, some, each.** Although there are exceptions, the following guidelines are generally reliable:

(a) **Everyone, everybody, anybody, anyone** invariably take singular verbs but may be referred to by either a singular or a plural pronoun.

Everyone brings **his** schedule cards to the bursar's office.

(*formal usage*)

Everyone brings **their** schedule cards to the bursar's office.

(*informal usage*)

(b) **All** and **some** are singular or plural according to the context. If the **of** phrase following the pronoun specifies a *mass* or *bulk* of something, the pronoun is singular; if the **of** phrase specifies a *number of things or persons,* the pronoun is plural.

Some of the fabric lost **its** coloring.

Some of the young men turned in **their** draft cards.

All of the draftees registered **their** complaints about the exemption procedure.

(c) **None** is singular or plural according to the context (the distinction in particular cases is sometimes so subtle that a writer could justify either one).

None of the young men **was** willing to turn in **his** draft card.

(*but* **were** . . . **their** *could also be justified in this case*)

Grammar

None of the young men in the hall **were** as tall as **their** fathers.

(*here it would be harder to justify the singular forms* **was** . . . **his**)

(d) **Each** is almost invariably singular.

Each of them declared **his** allegiance to democracy.

If you match up your pronouns in person, number, and gender with their antecedent nouns, you will make it easier for your reader to figure out what the pronouns refer to.

24

A pronoun should have a clear antecedent.

Examples of no antecedent or an unclear antecedent for the pronoun:

1 He retraced his steps to the bedroom, but **it** appeared to be hopeless.

(*what appeared to be hopeless?*)

2 John told his father that **his** car wouldn't start.

(*whose car? the father's or John's?*)

3 The word **deer** originally meant a wild animal, **which** first appeared in the twelfth century.

(*what first appeared in the twelfth century? the word* **deer**? *a wild animal? or* **meaning**?—*a word that is not in the previous clause*)

4 The league's first major step was to sponsor a cleanup day, but **it** could not enlist enough volunteers.

(*a pronoun should not refer to a noun functioning as a possessive or as a modifier—here* **league's**)

16

5 He is a strictly passive character, buffeted by fate, driven hither and yon, the unwilling pawn of forces stronger than himself. **This** makes him resent all offers of help.

(*this refers to an idea or a situation in the previous sentence, not to some noun in that sentence; but it is not even clear* **which** *idea or situation is being referred to*)

Careless handling of the pronoun often blocks communication between a writer and his reader. The writer always knows what he meant the pronoun to stand for, but if there is no noun in the previous group of words to which the pronoun can refer, or if it is difficult to find the noun to which the pronoun refers, the reader will not know, and will have to guess, what the pronoun stands for.

A good piece of advice for the apprentice writer is that whenever he uses a pronoun, he should check to see whether there is a noun in the previous group of words that he could put in the place of the pronoun. Let's apply this advice to the sentence "Mayor Worthington, acting on the advice of his physician, resigned the office of the president of the council, and the council, responding to a mandate from the voters, was swift to accept it." There are three neuter, singular nouns in the previous group of words to which the final pronoun **it** could refer: **advice, office, mandate.** But when we put each of these nouns, successively, in the place of **it,** we see that none of them names what the council accepted. If we pondered the sentence long enough, we might eventually figure out that what the council accepted was the mayor's **resignation.** But since there is no such noun in the previous group of words, the writer could avoid even a momentary vagueness if he would use the noun phrase **his resignation** instead of the pronoun **it.**

The use of the pronouns **this** and **that** to refer to a whole idea in a previous clause or sentence has been a common

Grammar

practice for a long time in spoken English, and this use is now becoming common in written English as well. Although this practice is gaining the approval of usage, a writer should be aware that by using the demonstrative pronouns **this** or **that** to refer to a whole idea in the previous clause or sentence he runs the risk that the reference of the pronoun will be vague or ambiguous for his readers. If he doesn't want to run that risk, he can use the **this** or **that** (or their corresponding plurals, **these** and **those**) as a demonstrative adjective modifying some summary noun. Thus, instead of saying, "I enjoyed the mountains, but this revealed to me that I really prefer a vacation at the beach," the writer may decide to protect his meaning by saying, "I enjoyed the mountains, but this experience revealed to me that I really prefer a vacation at the beach."

The use of the relative pronoun **which** to refer to a whole idea in the main clause rather than to a specific noun is also becoming more common and acceptable. But there is a risk in this use similar to the one that attends the use of **this** or **that** to refer to a whole idea. The writer who worries about whether his reader may be even momentarily baffled by the sentence "I decided to break the engagement with my girlfriend, which distressed my parents very much" will supply a summary noun to serve as the antecedent for **which**: "I decided to break the engagement with my girlfriend, a decision which distressed my parents very much."

The writer who has mastered the use of the pronoun has mastered a good part of the craft of writing lucid prose.

25

An introductory verbal or verbal phrase must find its "doer" in the subject of the main clause.

Examples of "dangling" verbal phrases:

1 Walking on the sidewalk, the Volkswagen ran over me.
2 By returning evil for evil, no permanent good can be accomplished.
3 Refusing to be inducted into the army, the World Boxing Association stripped Muhammad Ali of his title.
4 To accomplish this end, it is necessary for us to study grammar and usage.

In English, an introductory verbal or verbal phrase (participles, gerunds, and infinitives) naturally adheres to the subject of the main clause. When the subject of the main clause is not the "doer" of the action indicated in the verbal, we say that the verbal **dangles**—that it is not attached to the proper agent. By ignoring this basic principle of English grammar, a writer often produces a ludicrous sentence, like (1) above, and in all cases says what he did not intend to say.

To prevent dangling verbals, the writer should make sure that the subject of the main clause is the *doer* of the action specified in the preceding verbal. If the writers of the sample sentences above had observed this caution, they would have revised their sentences to read:

Grammar

1 Walking on the sidewalk, I was run over by a Volkswagen. **OR:** A Volkswagen ran over me while I was walking on the sidewalk.

2 By returning evil for evil, one can accomplish no permanent good.

3 Refusing to be inducted into the army, Muhammad Ali was stripped of his title by the World Boxing Association. **OR:** The World Boxing Association stripped Muhammad Ali of his title for refusing to be inducted into the army.

4 To accomplish this end, we must study grammar and usage.

26

Misplaced modifiers lead to a misreading of the sentence.

Examples of misplaced modifiers:

1 Anyone who reads a newspaper **frequently** will notice that many people are now concerned about pollution.

2 The author seems to be saying that people who refer to the past **constantly** follow the same ritual themselves.

3 He has **only** a face that a mother could love.

4 The teacher distributed examinations to the students **covered with splotches of ink.**

5 **After you entered the park,** the sponsors of the Summerfest decided that you would not have to spend any more money at the concession stands.

Because English is a language that depends heavily on word order, related words must often be placed as close as possible to one another. Adverbial and adjectival modifiers especially must be placed as close as possible to words that they modify. Failure to juxtapose related words often leads to a misreading, to a reading different from what the writer intended.

In the first two sample sentences above, we have examples

of what are called **squinting modifiers,** modifiers that look in two directions at once. In the first sentence, the adverb **frequently** is sitting between two verbs that grammatically and semantically it could modify—**reads** and **will notice.** If the writer intends the adverb to modify the act of reading rather than the act of noticing, he should shift the position of **frequently** so that the sentence reads as follows: **Anyone who frequently reads a newspaper will notice that many people are now concerned about pollution.** If, however, the writer intends the adverb to modify the act of noticing, he should shift **frequently** to a position between **will** and **notice** or after **notice.**

In the second sample sentence, the adverb **constantly** is likewise sitting between two verbs that it could modify—**refer** and **follow.** Shifting the adverb to a position before the verb **refer** will make the sentence say what the writer probably meant it to say: **The author seems to be saying that people who constantly refer to the past follow the same ritual themselves.**

Because **only** in the third sample sentence is placed in the wrong clause in the sentence, it modifies **a face.** The writer of that sentence could avoid eliciting chuckles from his readers if he would put **only** in the clause where it belongs and make his sentence read as follows: **He has a face that only a mother could love.**

Notice how shifting the position of the modifiers in the fourth and fifth sample sentences makes the sentences say what they were intended to say:

The teacher distributed to the students examinations covered with splotches of ink.

The sponsors of the Summerfest decided that after you entered the park you would not have to spend any more money at the concession stands.

Grammar

Reading sentences aloud will sometimes reveal the misplacement of modifying words, phrases, and clauses.

27

Preserve parallel structure by using units of the same grammatical kind.

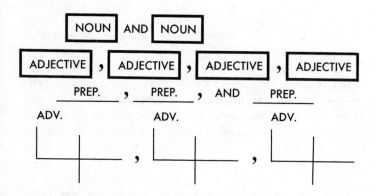

Examples of breakdown in parallelism:

1 The old beliefs about theft have been rejected as **superstitions** and **detrimental** to one's prestige.
   (*noun and adjective*)

2 He was a **miser**, a **bachelor**, and **egotistical**.
   (*noun, noun, adjective*)

3 John was **healthy**, **wealthy**, and an **athlete**.
   (*adjective, adjective, noun*)

4 Lincoln was a man **of the people**, **for the people**, and **loved by the people**.
   (*prepositional phrase, prepositional phrase, participial phrase*)

5 The President commended the steelworkers **for their patriotism** and **because they did not ask for a wage increase.**

(*prepositional phrase, adverb clause*)

6 The admen **not only** convince the reader that the Continental is a luxury car **but also** that the car confers status on its owner.

(*violation of parallelism with correlative conjunctions*)

The principle governing parallel structure is that a pair or a series (three or more) of coordinate units should be of the same kind—nouns with nouns, adjectives with adjectives, not a mixture of nouns and adjectives. A breakdown in parallelism wrenches coherence because it disrupts the expectation that is set up for a reader when a series starts out with one kind of unit and then suddenly shifts to another kind.

The obvious way to correct a breakdown in parallelism is to convert all the members of the pair or the series to units of the same grammatical kind. Sometimes a writer has an either/or choice for the conversion, as in the second sample sentence above: **He was a miser, a bachelor, and egotistical** (noun, noun, adjective). Here the writer has the option of converting all the units of the series into nouns (**He was a miser, a bachelor, and an egotist**) or into adjectives (**He was miserly, celibate, and egotistical**). Likewise, the writer of the fifth sample sentence above can convert both units of the pair into prepositional phrases (**for their patriotism** and **for their restraint** in not asking for a wage increase) or into adverb clauses (**because they were patriotic** and **because they did not ask for a wage increase**).

In the third sample sentence above, however, the writer does not have an either/or choice. He can convert the three predicate complements into adjectives (He was **healthy, wealthy,** and **athletic**), but since there is no noun equivalent of the adjective **healthy** (a **valetudinarian** is not quite right) nor a single-word noun equivalent of the adjective **wealthy** (he

23

Grammar

would have to use **a rich man**), he cannot convert all the complements into nouns.

It should be pointed out that although grammatical options are frequently available, one of the options will usually be stylistically preferable to the other. The writer has to exercise his judgment in making the better stylistic choice.

The breakdown in parallelism in the sixth sample sentence above is of a slightly different kind. This sample sentence illustrates a violation of parallelism when correlative conjunctions are used: **either . . . or; neither . . . nor; not (only) . . . but (also)**. The principle operating with correlative conjunctions is that **the same grammatical structure must be on the right-hand side of both conjunctions**. We can more easily see the breakdown in parallelism if we lay out the sixth sample sentence in two layers:

> The admen **not only** convince the reader that the Continental is
>   a luxury car
>   **but also** that the car confers status on its owner.

On the right-hand side of **not only** the writer has this grammatical sequence: a verb (**convince**), a noun (**the reader**), and a noun clause (**that the Continental is a luxury car**). On the right-hand side of **but also**, however, he has only the noun clause (**that the car confers status on its owner**). He can fix up the parallelism in either of two ways:

> The admen **not only** convince the reader that the Continental is
>   a luxury car
>   **but also** convince the reader that the car confers
>   status on its owner.
>   **OR** (probably preferable stylistically):
> The admen convince the reader **not only** that the Continental is
>   a luxury car
>   **but also** that the car confers
>   status on its owner.

In both revisions we now have the same grammatical structures on the right-hand side of both correlative conjunctions.

Note how parallelism is preserved in the following two sentences using correlative conjunctions:

> **Either** he will love the one and hate the other, **or** he will hate the one and love the other.

> He will **either** love the one and hate the other **or** hate the one and love the other.

The principle governing parallelism: **like must be yoked with like.**

28

Use the subordinate conjunction that if it will prevent a possible misreading.

Examples where it would be advisable to insert **that**:

1 My father believed‸his doctor, who was a boyhood friend, was wholly trustworthy.

2 A more realistic person would probably assert‸these statements about the ad were frivolous and sentimental.

3 He discovered‸the radio and the tape recorder in his roommate's closet had been stolen.

4 The author reported‸as soon as a Jew became intensely depressed in camp and lost all purpose for living, death came shortly after.

The tendency of any language is toward economy of means. So we elide syllables in such contractions as **he's, she'll, we'd, won't,** and we resort to such common elliptical expressions as **not all (of) the men; he is taller than I (am tall); when (I was) in the fourth grade, I went to the zoo with my father.** We also frequently omit the conjunction **that** which introduces

Grammar

a noun clause serving as the object of a verb, as in "He said he was going" and "He announced I was a candidate for office."

Whether to use the conjunction **that** in written prose will be a problem only when a noun clause is being used as the direct object of a verb—but not in every instance of such use. If there is no chance that the syntax of a sentence will be misread, it is all right, even in written prose, to omit **that**. But if there is a chance that a noun phrase following the verb may be read as the object of the verb rather than as the subject of the subsequent clause, then the writer should prevent even a momentary misreading by inserting **that** at the head of the noun clause. What follows may make all of this clearer.

In a sentence like **He said he was going,** it is safe to omit **that** after **said** because **he,** being a pronoun in the nominative case, cannot possibly be read as the object of **said.** But in a sentence like the first sample sentence above, it is not only possible but likely that the noun phrase **his doctor** will momentarily be read as the object of **believed (he believed his doctor).** Of course, as soon as the reader comes on the predicate **was wholly trustworthy,** he realizes that he has misread the sentence, and he has to back up and reread the sentence as the writer intended it to be read. But the writer could have prevented that initial misreading by inserting **that** after **believed**—My father believed **that** his doctor, who was a boyhood friend, was wholly trustworthy. Then the sentence can be read in only one way—the way in which the writer intended it to be read.

Note how the insertion of **that** where the caret is in the other sample sentences prevents an initial misreading of the sentences. Whenever a reader has to reread a sentence in order to make sense of it, the writer is usually the one to blame. Inserting **that** where it is necessary or advisable will save the reader from having to reread a sentence.

29

**Avoid the careless or indefensible use of
sentence fragments.**

Examples of questionable sentence fragments:

1 The reason for this reaction being that people are flattered by courtesy.

2 I shall not try to defend myself on the grounds that I did not violate the regulation. **Although I could offer the excuse that I didn't know that such a regulation existed.**

3 Both men are alike in that they try to help people only if the effort does not result in too much trouble for themselves. **Herenger, in his idea that it is good to help someone with ''so little trouble to himself,'' and the Baron, who believes in giving money to someone as long as there is no further responsibility involved.**

4 The bond between Gretta and Michael was strong enough to make him face death rather than be separated from her. **The tragedy here that such a love could not be consummated and that one so young should be cut off just at the dawn of life.**

5 Much information about a topic can be brought forth by poetry. **The topic of science, in particular, because science is basically factual.**

A sentence fragment can be defined as a string of words, between an initial capital letter and a period or question mark, that lacks a subject or a finite-verb predicate (or both) or that has a subject and a finite-verb predicate but is made part of a larger structure by a relative pronoun (**who, which, that**) or by a subordinating conjunction (**because, if, when,** etc.).

The bold string of words in the first example above is a sentence fragment because the subject **reason** lacks a finite-verb predicate. Changing the participle **being** to the finite verb **is** would make that string of words a complete sentence.

The bold string of words in the second example is a sentence fragment because the subordinating conjunction **although** makes the clause that follows it a part of, or dependent on, a larger structure. The adverb clause introduced by **although** "depends on" the independent clause in the previous sentence, and therefore the adverb clause cannot stand by itself. This example may be more the result of carelessness in punctuating the sentence than the result of ignorance of what constitutes a complete sentence, for the sentence fragment here can be eliminated simply by changing the period after **regulation** to a comma and reducing the first letter in **Although** to lowercase (**I shall not try to defend myself on the grounds that I did not violate the regulation, although I could offer the excuse that I didn't know that such a regulation existed**).

The bold string of words in the third example is a sentence fragment because it lacks an independent clause. It lacks an independent clause because neither **Herenger** nor **Baron,** which appear to be "subjects," has a predicate verb. Likewise, **The tragedy** in the fourth example and **The topic of science** in the fifth lack predicate verbs.

Whether a string of words constitutes a complete sentence or only a sentence fragment is a grammatical concern; whether the use of a sentence fragment is appropriate in a particular context and is therefore justifiable is a rhetorical or stylistic concern. It is a fact of life that sometimes we communicate with one another in sentence fragments. Take for instance the following exchange:

Where are you going tonight?
The movies.
With whom?

Jack.
Where?
The Palace.
What time?
About 8:30.
By car?
No, by bus.
Can I go along?
Sure.

Once the context of that dialogue was established, both speakers communicated with one another in fragments. Notice, though, that the dialogue had to be initiated by a complete sentence (the question **Where are you going tonight?**) and that later the first speaker had to resort again to a complete sentence **(Can I go along?)** because there was no way to phrase that question clearly in a fragmentary way.

Native speakers of a language can converse in fragments because each of them is capable of mentally supplying what is missing from an utterance. When in response to the initial question the second speaker answers, "The movies," that phrase conveys a meaning because the first speaker is able to supply, mentally and perhaps subconsciously, the missing elements in the fragmentary reply: **(I am going to) the movies.**

All of us have encountered sentence fragments in the written prose of some very reputable writers. Predicateless sentences are most likely to be found in mood-setting descriptive and narrative prose, as in this first paragraph of Charles Dickens's novel *Bleak House:*

London. Michaelmas Term lately over, and the Lord Chancellor sitting in Lincoln's Inn Hall. Implacable November weather. As much mud in the streets, as if the waters had but newly retired from the face of the earth, and it would not be wonderful to meet a Megalosaurus, forty feet long or so, waddling like an elephantine lizard up Holborn Hill. Smoke lowering down from chimney-pots, making a soft black drizzle, with flakes of soot in it as big as full-grown snow-flakes—gone into mourning, one might imagine, for the death of the sun. Dogs, undistinguishable in mire. Horses, scarcely better; splashed to their blinkers. Foot passengers, jostling one another's umbrellas, in a general infection of ill-temper, and losing their foothold at street-corners, where tens of thousands of other foot passengers have been slipping and sliding since the day broke (if this day ever broke), adding new deposits to the crust upon crust of mud, sticking at those points tenaciously to the pavement and accumulating at compound interest.

In that paragraph, there are a few clauses (that is, groups of words with a subject and a finite-verb predicate), but the paragraph is composed predominantly of nouns and noun phrases, some of them modified by participial phrases. But although the passage is largely lacking in predications made by finite verbs, the sequence of sentence fragments creates effects that Dickens could not have achieved—or could not have achieved as well—with complete sentences.

The point of citing these examples of spoken and written discourse is that sentence fragments are a part of the English language (in that sense they are "grammatical"), that in certain contexts they do communicate meaning, and that in some circumstances and for some purposes they are appropriate and therefore acceptable, effective, and even stylistically desirable. But the writer should be aware of what he is doing. He should know that he is writing a sentence fragment rather than a complete sentence; otherwise he will be guilty of a *careless* use of a sentence fragment. And he should have some purpose or effect in mind when he uses a sentence fragment; otherwise he will be guilty of an *indefensible* use of a sentence fragment.

30

Independent clauses cannot be spliced together simply with a comma.

Examples of comma splices:

1 We are not allowed to think for ourselves, that privilege is reserved for administrators.

2 Last summer my family saw the whole United States from the inside
of an air-conditioned trailer, outside the weather ranged from
cool to hot, from dry to muggy.

3 Our minds are never challenged by the television set, it is just
so much easier to sit there than to read a book.

4 You will have to choose your vocation yourself, however, you
should consider what others have told you about the hazards of
various jobs.

A comma splice is the joining of independent clauses with a
comma. It occurs only in compound sentences—that is, in
sentences composed of two or more independent clauses. A
comma splice is an error in punctuation, but since punctuation
is, for the written language, the equivalent of vocal intonation
in the spoken language, this error in punctuation can also be
considered an error in grammar.

Independent clauses must be joined either by a coordinating
conjunction (**and, but, or, for, yet, so**) or by a semicolon.
In addition to these two ways of properly splicing independent
clauses, there are two other ways of fixing up the comma
splice: by making separate sentences of the two clauses and

31

Grammar

by subordinating one of the clauses. Using each of these methods in turn, let us correct the comma splice in the first sample sentence above:

(a) Insert the appropriate coordinating conjunction after the comma:

We are not allowed to think for ourselves, **for** that privilege is reserved for administrators.

(b) Substitute a semicolon for the comma:

We are not allowed to think for ourselves; that privilege is reserved for administrators.

(c) Subordinate one of the independent clauses:

We are not allowed to think for ourselves, **because** that privilege is reserved for administrators.

(d) Put a period at the end of the first independent clause and begin a new sentence with the first word of the second independent clause:

We are not allowed to think for ourselves. That privilege is reserved for administrators.

Although these four ways of fixing up a comma splice are always available, one of these options will usually be better in a particular instance. In the case of the first sample sentence, splicing the two clauses together with a semicolon would probably be best: **We are not allowed to think for ourselves; that privilege is reserved for administrators.** The semicolon here effects the closest union of the two related clauses and best points up the irony between the thoughts in the two clauses. We have made our choice of the semicolon on stylistic grounds; grammatically, the other three options are equally correct.

See **66** and **67** in the punctuation section for the proper use of the semicolon.

31

Do not run independent clauses together without a conjunction or the proper punctuation.

Examples of independent clauses run together:

1 Why am I qualified to speak on this subject I just finished three dreadful years of high school.

2 Those shiny red apples sitting on my desk pleased me very much they were tokens of affection from my students.

3 Two suspects were arrested last week one of them was a cripple.

4 Leggatt was blackballed for having killed a man thus he would never be able to work on a ship again.

The term commonly used to label two or more independent clauses that have been run together without any conjunction or punctuation is **fused sentence** or **run-on sentence.** Fused sentences are not as common in writing as comma splices, but when they do occur, they are even more of a stumbling block for a reader than comma splices are. If the writers of the sample sentences above had read their string of words aloud, they would have detected a natural stopping place—a place where the expression of one thought ended and the expression of another thought began.

Fused sentences can be corrected in the same four ways that comma splices can be corrected:

(a) Join the independent clauses with the appropriate coordinating conjunction:

Those shiny red apples sitting on my desk pleased me very much, **for** they were tokens of affection from my students.

Grammar

(b) Splice the independent clauses with a semicolon:

Two suspects were arrested last week; one of them was a cripple.

(c) Subordinate one of the independent clauses:

Because Leggatt was blackballed for having killed a man, he would never be able to work on a ship again.

(d) Make separate sentences of the independent clauses:

Why am I qualified to speak on this subject? I just finished three dreadful years of high school.

As in the case of comma splices, all four of these ways are usually available for correcting a fused sentence, but in a particular instance, one of them will usually be better than the others. Some of the sample sentences do not readily lend themselves to correction by all four means. For instance, because the first sample sentence fuses a question and a statement—**Why am I qualified to speak on this subject** (question) and **I just finished three dreadful years of high school** (statement)—it lends itself to correction only by the fourth method, that of making separate sentences of the two clauses.

Reading one's prose aloud will usually disclose instances where independent clauses have been run together.

32

Choose words and put them together so that they make sense.

Examples of confused or puzzling sentences:

1 This same technique of philosophical truths expressed tersely and lyrically, which we often see in Johnson's works, is very prevalent in *Rasselas*.

2 Much later in the story, the dinner conversation the function of the "small talk" seems to be about the old times.

3 The youth, rejected by his parents, by the world, by God, and tragically and ultimately he has rejected himself.

4 William Faulkner presents in his short story "Barn Burning" a human character that is as nonhuman as is feasible to a person's mind.

5 Now in the third stanza, the poet starts his descent. He brings about his conclusion of the boy, which can be paralleled to mankind.

6 Of course, this situation of rundown houses is not always the case, but instead the high rent that the tenants have to pay, which leaves little money for anything else.

A confused or puzzling sentence is one that because of some flaw in the choice or disposition of words reveals no meaning or only a vague meaning. We could say of such a sentence that it is a "non-English" sentence—a sentence that is semantically or grammatically impossible in the English language. A sentence like "The ice cube froze" is a non-English sentence because the meanings of **ice cube** and **froze** are incompatible. We can say, "The water froze," but we are uttering "nonsense" if we say, "The ice cube froze." The phrase **his conclusion of the boy** in the fifth sample sentence above is an instance of a choice of incompatible words. A sentence like "Harshly me teacher scolded the yesterday" is a non-English sentence because English grammar does not allow that order of words. To make sense, those words have to be disposed in an order like this: **The teacher scolded me harshly yesterday.** Each of the first, second, third, and sixth sample sentences has some flaw in syntax that prevents the writer's meaning from getting through to the reader.

If the reader cannot figure out what the writer meant to

say, he often cannot even analyze what went wrong with the sentence, and he certainly cannot suggest to the writer how the bewildering sentence might be fixed up. He can only point out to the writer that the sentence makes no sense and urge him to try again to say what he meant to say.

What were the writers of the sample sentences trying to say?

Style

Style is the result of the choices that a writer makes from the available vocabulary and syntactical resources of a language. A writer may not choose—or should not choose

☐ **Words and structures that are not part of the language:**

The defendants have **klinded** the case to the Supreme Court. (*no such word in the English language*)

All gas stations **have being closed** for the duration of the emergency.
(*no such verb structure in the English language*)

☐ **Words and structures that make no sense:**

The mountains lucidly transgressed sentient rocks. (*a grammatical but nonsensical sentence*)

☐ **Words and structures that do not convey a clear, unambiguous meaning:**

The teacher gave the papers to the students that were chosen by the committee.

(*was it the **papers** or the **students** that were chosen by the committee?*)

Style

Aside from these unavailable or inadvisable choices, however, the rich vocabulary and the flexible syntax of the English language offer the writer a number of alternative but synonymous ways of saying something. A writer may choose to use an active verb or a passive verb:

He reported the accident to the police.

OR: The accident was reported by him to the police.

or he may shift the position of some modifiers:

He reported the accident to the police when he was ready.

OR: When he was ready, he reported the accident to the police.

or he may substitute synonymous words and phrases:

He informed the police about the accident at the intersection.

OR: John notified Sergeant James Murphy about the collision at the corner of Fifth and Main.

A number of other stylistic choices may be open to the writer. For instance, he may have to decide whether to write a long sentence or to break up the sentence into a series of separate short sentences; whether to write a compound sentence or to subordinate one of the clauses; whether to modify a noun with an adjective clause or with a participial phrase or with merely an adjective; whether to use literal language or figurative language; whether to use a "big" word or a simple word (*altercation* or *quarrel*), a specific word or a general word (*sauntered* or *walked*), a formal word or a colloquial word (*children* or *kids*).

Grammar will determine whether a stylistic choice is *correct*—that is, whether a particular locution is allowable by the conventions of the language. Rhetoric will determine whether a stylistic choice is *effective*—that is, whether a particular locution conveys the intended meaning with the clarity, economy, emphasis, and tone appropriate to the subject matter, occasion, audience, and desired effect.

This section on style asks the writer to consider whether he has made the best choice of words or arrangement of words. Questions about style are not so much questions about *right* and *wrong* as questions about *good, better, best*.

40

Choose the right word for what you intend to say.

Examples of wrong words:

1 The typical surfer has long **ignominious** hair bleached by the **torpid** sun.

2 By the time we reached Phoenix, we had spent our food allotment and were faced with the gloomy **aspect** of starving to death.

3 If you do not **here** from me within three weeks, give me a call.

4 The shortstop played very **erotically** in the first game of the doubleheader.

A word is labeled "wrong" when its meaning does not fit the context, does not express the intended meaning. The most obvious instance of a "wrong word" is the substitution, usually due to carelessness, of a homonym (a like-sounding word) for the intended word, like **here** for **hear** (see the third example above), **through** for **threw**, **there** for **their**, **sole** for **soul**.

Another kind of "wrong word" is what is called a **malapropism**, after Mrs. Malaprop in Sheridan's eighteenth-century play *The Rivals*. Mrs. Malaprop would say things like "as headstrong as an *allegory* on the banks of the Nile." There is a malapropism in the fourth example above. The writer has heard the expression "he played erratically," but by using the approximate-sounding word **erotically**, he has produced a

Style

"howler." **Aspect** in the second example above makes some sense, but *prospect* would come closer to expressing what the writer probably had in mind.

The most common kind of "wrong word" is usually the result of a writer's using a word that is new and somewhat unfamiliar to him. In the first example above, the denotative meaning of **ignominious** is "disgraceful, shameful," but although we can speak of "an ignominious act," the word is inappropriate when attached to **hair.** In the same sentence, if the writer meant to say that the sun was sluggish, **torpid** is the right word; but "torrid sun" comes closer to what he probably meant to say.

Until a writer gains the assured familiarity with words that will prevent the choice of the wrong word for what he intends to say, he would do well to consult a dictionary whenever he is prompted to use a word that has not been part of his working vocabulary.

41

Choose the precise word for what you want to say.

Examples of imprecise words:

1 I liked the movie *Love Story* because it was **beautiful.**
2 What most impressed me about the poem was the poet's **descriptive** language.
3 Has-been athletes always have a **sore** look on their face.
4 To prevent her from catching a cold, he insisted that she wear the **gigantic** galoshes.

Whereas a "wrong word" misses the target entirely, an "imprecise word" hits all around the bull's-eye but never on dead center.

The word **beautiful** in the first example above is too general to convey a precise meaning. A reader's response to a general word like that would be to ask, "In what way was the movie beautiful?" If the writer had said "poignant" or "believable" or "edifying" or "inspiring" or "visually pleasing," the reader might want some more particulars, but at least he would have a clearer idea of why the writer liked the movie.

The word **descriptive** in the second example is too vague. Expressions like "the poet's vivid, sensory diction" or "the poet's simple, concrete words" or "the poet's specific adjectives for indicating colors" would give the reader a more exact idea of the kind of descriptive language that impressed the writer of the sentence.

Sore in the third example is ambiguous—that is, it has more than one meaning in the context. If the writer wants to convey the notion that the former athletes were disgruntled, let him say that "they have an angry look on their face" or simply that "they look angry," but if he wants to convey the notion that the former athletes exhibited physical discomfort, let him say that "they have a painful look on their face"—or in some other way say that their faces reflect their aching wounds.

Gigantic in the fourth example is hyperbolic, or exaggerated. Unless the writer of that sentence deliberately used the hyperbolic **gigantic** for humorous effect, he should use a more proportionate word like *big* or *heavy* or *ungainly*.

In the spoken medium, we often do not have the leisure to search for the precise word; we utter the first word that offers itself. In response to the question "How did you like him?" we might say, "Oh, I thought he was nice enough." If the person with whom we are speaking is not satisfied by our general word of approval, *nice,* he can ask us to be more specific. In the written medium, however, the situation is quite different: we do have the leisure to search for a precise word, and we are not available to the reader who may want more

Style

specific information. Consulting a thesaurus or, better yet, a dictionary that discriminates the meanings of synonyms will frequently yield the exact word for our intended meaning.

42

Choose words that are appropriate to the context.

Examples of inappropriate words:

1 Before the unbelieving **orbs** of the other players, he advances his piece on the board, arresting his **manual appendage** only when he sees that he is going to land on Boardwalk.

2 With **mendacious sangfroid,** he remarked, "You don't have to apologize. I've known lots of people who have done it," and in the same **prevaricating** tone, he **asseverates,** "Virtue is as virtue does."

3 The conclusion that I have come to is that **kids** should not have to suffer for the sins of their fathers.

4 My senator tries to act **real groovy and all,** but despite all the **mod rags** he affects, he still gives out with all that graybeard **jive** about the importance of getting a good education so that you can get a good job so that you can afford to maintain a prestigious **pad** and **wheels.**

A word is inappropriate to its context if it does not fit, if it is out of tune with, the subject matter, the occasion, the audience, or the personality of the speaker or writer. It is conspicuous by its inharmonious presence.

No word in isolation can be labeled "inappropriate"; it must be seen in the company of other words before it can be declared "inappropriate." Although one would feel safer in making a judgment if one had a larger context, the italicized words in the first two examples above seem to be inappropriate because they are too elegant or inflated for the subject matter—a game of Monopoly in the first sentence, a reporting of a remark made at a cocktail party in the second sentence. There seems to be no good reason for the writer of the first sentence not to use the simpler, less pretentious *eyes* for **orbs** and *hand* for **manual appendage.** Young writers consciously striving to enlarge their vocabulary often produce sentences like the second example. Instead of using a thesaurus to find an accurate or precise word for what they want to say, they use it to find an unusual or a polysyllabic word that will make their prose sound ''literary.'' The one hopeful thing that can be said about such writers is that if they are ambitious enough to want to expand their working vocabulary, they will very soon develop enough sophistication about language to know when it is appropriate, and when it is inappropriate, to use ''big words.''

The more common fault of inappropriateness, however, is diction that is too colloquial, too slangy, for its formal context. Although there are contexts where the colloquial **kids** would be more appropriate than the word *children,* the third example above seems not to be one of those contexts. There are contexts where slang and even the jargon of particular social groups will be perfectly appropriate, but the slang in the fourth sample sentence above seems to be out of tune with the subject matter and with the majority of the other words in the sentence. Even if the writer of that sentence could justify the use of such terms as **groovy, mod rags,** and **jive** as being appropriate to his personality, he could not justify the use of **pad** and **wheels** in that part of the sentence where apparently he is paraphrasing the pious platitudes of his senator. Even if the senator had been addressing a group of hippies, he would not have used **pad** for *home* or **wheels** for *automobile.*

Style

Since dictionaries, thesauruses, and handbooks will not be of much help in telling a writer when a word is appropriate, the writer will have to rely on the criteria of subject matter, occasion, audience, desired effect, and personality of the author. Another way to put the precept is to say that the writer's "voice" must remain consistent with the overall tone he has established in a particular piece of writing.

43

Use the proper idiom.

Examples of lapse of idiom:

1 Although I agree **to** a few of Socrates' principles, I must disagree **to** many of them.

2 Conformity has been a common tendency throughout **the** American history.

3 Blake then **differs** the two introductory pieces by contrasting the simplicity and innocence of the child with the maturity and sophistication of the adult.

4 Harold and the star quarterback from Steuben High also **compared very much** in being able to throw a clothesline pass.

5 Abner had no interest or respect **for** the boy.

To label a locution "unidiomatic" is to indicate that native speakers of the language do not say it that way—in any dialect of the language. Surprisingly, unidiomatic expressions are one of the commonest weaknesses to be found in the prose of unpracticed writers. Why do lapses of idiom occur so frequently? They occur often because many writers have not paid close enough attention—have not attuned their ears—to the way native speakers of the language, including themselves, say something. In trying to express themselves on paper, they put down expressions that they would never use in the spoken medium and that they have never heard any other native speaker use.

No native speaker of the English language, for instance, would use the article **the** in the phrase **throughout the American history** (see the second example above). However, an American speaker would say "He was in the hospital," whereas a British speaker would say "He was in hospital." Oriental students, especially the Japanese and Chinese, have trouble with the English article, because their language does not use a part of speech like our article.

Lapses of idiom frequently occur with prepositions. A number of prepositions fit idiomatically with the verb **agree,** but the writer must attune his ear to the proper idiom in the proper place. He can say **agree to** in an expression like "He agreed to the conditions we laid down." He can say **agree on** in an expression like "They can't agree on the wording of the proposal." The preposition that fits idiomatically with the sense of **agree** in the first example above is **with:** "I agree **with** a few of Socrates' principles" and "I disagree **with** many of them."

Unidiomatic prepositions often appear in compounded phrases, as in the fifth example above. The preposition **for** does fit with **respect** ("respect for the boy"), but it does not fit with **interest** ("interest for the boy"). In such cases, the idiomatic preposition must be inserted for both members of the compound, e.g. "Abner had no interest **in,** or respect **for,** the boy."

In phrasing the third and fourth sentences above, native speakers would say "Blake then **differentiates** the two introductory pieces . . ." and "Harold and the star quarterback from Steuben High were also **comparable** in their ability to throw . . ."

Style

What prevents a handbook from setting reliable guidelines for proper idioms is that logic plays little or no part in establishing idiom. If logic played such a part, we would say "He looked *down* the word in the dictionary" instead of "He looked *up* the word in the dictionary. Although the eye normally runs down the columns of a dictionary when searching for a word, native speakers say "look up" a word simply because that is the way people have always phrased that locution. An editor or an instructor can call your attention to an unidiomatic expression and insert the correct idiom, but he cannot give you any rule that will prevent other lapses of idiom. You simply have to learn proper idioms by reading more and by listening more intently.

44

Avoid trite expressions.

Examples of trite expressions:

1 I returned from the picnic **tired but happy,** and that night I slept **like a log.**
2 My primary objective in coming to college was to get a **well-rounded education.**
3 The construction of two new hotels was a **giant step forward** for the community.
4 In the last few years, the popularity of ice hockey has grown **by leaps and bounds.**
5 Convinced now that drugs are a temptation for young people, the community must **nip the problem in the bud** before it **runs rampant.**

There is nothing grammatically or idiomatically wrong with a trite expression. A trite expression is stylistically objectionable—mainly because it is a *tired* expression. Whether or not an expression is "tired" is, of course, a relative matter. What is a cliché for some readers may be bright-penny new for others. But it would be surprising if the expressions in the examples above were not jaded for most readers.

Trite expressions are combinations of words that have been used so often that they have lost their freshness and even their meaning for most readers. Metaphors are especially prone to staleness. Metaphors like "nip in the bud," "slept like a log," "giant step" were once fresh and cogent; they are now wilted.

Overworked combinations like "a well-rounded education" should be banished from the language, partly because they are boring and partly because they no longer convey a precise meaning. Someone should be daring enough to mint the expression "a well-squared education" and see whether it gains currency.

Be wary of weary words.

45

Rephrase awkwardly constructed sentences.

Examples of awkward sentences:

1 You could get a dose of the best exercise a person could undertake, walking. I believe a person should walk at a leisurely pace, with no set goal on distance.

2 The football player has had many broken noses, with which he ends up looking like a prizefighter.

3 I and probably everybody else who started drinking beer in their sophomore year of high school thought the only thing to do was get drunk and go to school activities where we could meet and have a good time.

Style

Awkward sentences are sentences so ineptly put together that the resultant jumble of words is difficult to read or understand. An awkward sentence is often the result of a writer's saying something in a wordy, roundabout way rather than in a terse, direct way. The problem is that the one who writes an awkwardly constructed sentence is usually not aware that he has done so; he has to be told that his sentence is awkward.

The ear, however, is a reliable resource for detecting awkward sentences. If a writer adopts the practice of reading his sentences aloud, he will often detect clumsy, odd-sounding combinations of words. Alerted by his ear, he should look for the usual causes of awkwardness: excessive verbiage, words and phrases out of their normal order, successions of prepositional phrases ("the president of the largest chapter of the national fraternity of students of dentistry"), pretentious circumlocutions ("the penultimate month of the year" for "November"), split constructions ("I, chastened by my past experiences, resolved to never consciously and maliciously circulate, even if true, damaging reports about my friends"), successions of rhyming words ("He tries wisely to revise the evidence supplied by his eyes"). In his effort to rephrase the sentence, the writer should try expressing the same thought in the way he would if he were *speaking* the sentence to someone.

The sample sentences above are awkward for a variety of reasons, but what they all have in common is excessive verbiage. Pruning some of the deadwood, rearranging some of the parts, using simpler, more idiomatic phrases, we can improve the articulation of those clumsy sentences:

1 Walking is the best exercise. A person should walk at a leisurely pace and only as far as he feels like going.
2 The football player has broken his nose so often that he looks like a prizefighter.

3 Like everybody else who started drinking beer in his sophomore year of high school, I thought that getting drunk was the best way to have a good time at school activities.

46

Cut out unnecessary words.

Examples of wordy sentences:

1 He was justified in trying to straighten out his mother on her backward ideas about her attitude toward Negroes. (19 words)

2 In this modern world of today, we must get an education that will prepare us for a job in our vocation in life. (23 words)

3 In the "Garden of Love," the poem relates the sad experience of a child being born into a cruel world. (20 words)

4 The meaning, at least in my own eyes, that he is trying to convey in the poem "Arms and the Boy" is of the evilness of war in that it forces innocent people to take up the instruments of death and destruction and then tries to teach them to love to use them to kill other human beings. (58 words)

A "wordy sentence" is one in which a writer has used more words than are needed to say what he wanted to say. A writer would soon learn to cultivate restraint if he were charged for every word used, as he is when he sends a telegram. He should not, of course, strive for a "telegraphic style" or a "headline style," but he should value words so much that he spends them sparingly.

Let us see if we can trim the sample sentences without substantially altering their meaning:

1 He was justified in trying to straighten out his mother's attitude toward Negroes. (13 words)

Style

2 In the modern world, we must get an education that will prepare us for a job. (16 words)

3 The "Garden of Love" relates the sad experience of a child being born into a cruel world. (17 words)

4 As I see it, the poet's thesis in "Arms and the Boy" is that war is evil because it not only forces people to take up arms but makes them use these weapons to kill other human beings. (38 words)

Notice that each of the revised sentences uses fewer words than the original. The retrenchment ranges from three words to twenty words. If the writers were being charged five cents a word, they could probably find other superfluous words to prune. The writer of the fourth sentence, for instance, would probably lop off **As I see it** and **in 'Arms and the Boy,'** and he would condense **to kill other human beings** to **to kill others.**

One should not become obsessed with saving words, but one should seize every opportunity of clearing out obvious deadwood. As Alexander Pope said,

> Words are like leaves, and where they most abound,
> Much fruit of sense beneath is rarely found.

47

Avoid careless repetition of words and ideas.

Examples of careless repetition:

1 Mr. Bucks, a **fellow colleague,** offered to intercede with the dean.

2 He does not rely on the **surrounding environment** as much as his brother does.

3 The objective point of view accentuates the emotional intensity of the love affair and the **impending** failure that will **eventually happen.**

4 There are some striking similarities between Segal and Hemingway, for **both** have studied life and love and found them **both** to be failures.

A "careless repetition" refers to the needless repetition of the same word in the same sentence (or in adjoining sentences) or to the juxtaposition of synonymous words that produces what is called a **redundancy** or a **tautology.**

The repetition of the pronoun **both** in the fourth example above is especially careless because the repeated pronouns have different antecedents (the first one refers to **Segal** and **Hemingway,** the second to **life** and **love**). The emphasis in this caution about the repetition of the same word should be put on the word *needless.* Sometimes it is better to repeat the same word, even in the same sentence, than to run the risk of ambiguity or misunderstanding. In a sentence like "She told her mother that her hairdryer was broken," if the ambiguity of the second **her** could not be remedied in some other way, it would be better to repeat the noun—e.g. "She told her **mother** that the **mother's** hairdryer was broken." In this case, however, there is a better way to avoid the ambiguity of the pronoun, namely by putting the sentence in direct discourse: "She told her mother, 'Your hairdryer is broken'" or "She told her mother, 'My hairdryer is broken.'"

The italicized words in the first three examples above are instances of redundancy or tautology (needless repetition of the same idea in different words). **Fellow** and **colleague, surrounding** and **environment, impending** and **eventually happen** are examples of repetitions of the same idea in different words. In the first two instances, drop the first italicized word; in the third, drop the whole **that** clause.

Repetition of key words can be an effective means of achieving coherence (see **61,** dealing with paragraph coherence, in the next section). What you are being cautioned about here is redundant and unnecessary repetition of words and ideas.

48

Avoid mixed metaphors.

Examples of mixed metaphors:

1 Sarty finally comes to the point where his inner turmoil reaches its **zenith** and **stagnates in a pool** of lethargy.

2 In "The Dead," James Joyce uses small talk as an effective **weapon** to **illustrate** his thesis.

3 He tried to **scale the wall** of indifference between them but found that he couldn't **burrow** through it.

4 For as long as Poe could remember, a **shadow** of guilt **hovered** over his head.

A mixed metaphor is the result of a writer's failure to keep a consistent image in his mind. All metaphors are based on the perceived likenesses between two things that exist in a different order of being—as for instance between a *man* and a *greyhound* ("The lean shortstop is a greyhound when he runs the bases"), *fame* and a *spur* ("Fame is the spur to ambition"), *mail* and an *avalanche* ("The mail buried the staff under an avalanche of complaints"). Whenever any detail is incompatible with one or other of the terms of the analogy, the metaphor is said to be "mixed."

Zenith, as in the first example above, connotes something skyrocketing, and therefore that detail is incompatible with the detail of stagnation. It is also difficult to reconcile the notion of **turmoil** with a **stagnant pool;** turmoil connotes violent movement, but a pool is static.

A **weapon** is not used to **illustrate** something. If one were climbing (**scaling**) a wall, one could not dig (**burrow**) through it at the same time. And anyone who has ever observed a **shadow** knows that it never **hovers** over a person's head.

Forming and maintaining a clear picture of the notion one is attempting to express figuratively will ensure a consistent metaphor.

49

Consider whether an active verb would be preferable to a passive verb.

Examples of questionable use of the passive voice:

1 Money **was borrowed** by the couple so that they could pay off all their bills.

2 His love for her **is shown** by his accepting her story and by his remaining at her side when she is in trouble.

3 From these recurrent images of hard, resistant metals, it **can be inferred** by us that he was a mechanical, heartless person.

4 Talking incessantly, he **was overwhelmed** by the girl.

The passive voice of the verb is a legitimate and useful part of the English language. A sentence using a passive verb as its predicate is a different but synonymous way of expressing the thought conveyed by a sentence using an active verb. The basic formula for a sentence using an active-verb construction is as follows:

NOUN PHRASE$_1$ + VERB + NOUN PHRASE$_2$

The judge   pronounced   the verdict

Style

The formula for transforming that active-verb construction into a passive-verb construction is as follows:

$$\text{NOUN PHRASE}_2 \; + \; \text{AUXILIARY} \; + \; \underset{\substack{\text{(past participle} \\ \text{form)}}}{\text{VERB}} \; + \; \textbf{by} \; + \; \text{NOUN PHRASE}_1$$

The verdict   was   pronounced   **by**   the judge

Notice the changes that have taken place in the second sentence: (1) Noun Phrase$_1$ and Noun Phrase$_2$ have switched positions, and (2) two words have been added, the auxiliary **was** and the preposition **by**. Although the second sentence expresses the same thought as the first sentence, it is longer, by two words, than the first sentence.

If the use of a passive verb is questionable, it is questionable only stylistically; that is, one can question the *choice* of a passive verb rather than an active verb in a particular instance. When someone does question the use of the passive verb, he is merely asking the writer to consider whether the sentence would not be more emphatic, more economical, less awkward, and somehow "neater" if he used an active verb. Challenged to consider the options available in a particular case, the writer still has the privilege of making the choice that seems better to him.

The writers of the first three sample sentences above should consider whether their sentences would be improved by the use of an active verb, as in these revisions:

1 The couple **borrowed** money so that they could pay off all their bills.

2 He **shows** his love for her by accepting her story and by remaining at her side when she is in trouble.

3 From these recurrent images of hard, resistant metals, we **can infer** that he was a mechanical, heartless person.

The writer of the first sentence might argue that he wanted to give special emphasis to **money,** and so he made **money** the subject of the sentence and put the word in the emphatic lead-off position in the sentence (**money was borrowed** . . .). A writer can also justify his use of a passive verb when he does not know the agent of an action or prefers not to reveal the agent or considers it unnecessary to indicate the agent, as in the sentence ''The story was reported to all the newspapers.''

Dangling verbals often result from the use of a passive-verb construction in the main clause (see **25** on dangling verbals). The writer of the fourth sentence in the examples above (**Talking incessantly, he was overwhelmed by the girl**) may not have a choice available to him. The context of that sentence suggests that the lead-off participial phrase (**talking incessantly**) may be dangling—that is, that it was not the boy (**he**) but the girl who was talking incessantly. If that is the case, the writer may not choose the passive verb rather than the active verb; he must use the active verb:

4 Talking incessantly, the girl overwhelmed him.

Paragraphing

One way to regard paragraphing is to view it as a system of punctuating stages of thought presented in units larger than the word and the sentence. Paragraphing is a means of alerting readers to a shift of focus in the development of the main idea of the whole discourse. It marks off for the reader's convenience the discrete but related parts of the whole discourse. How paragraphing facilitates reading would be made dramatically evident if a whole discourse were written or printed—as ancient manuscripts once were—in a single, unbroken block.

Like punctuation and mechanics, paragraphing is a feature only of the written language. Some linguists claim that speakers of connected discourse signal their "paragraphs" by pauses and by shifts in the tone of their voice. (The next time you hear a speech being delivered from a written text, see if you can detect when the speaker shifts to another paragraph of his manuscript.) But speakers are not conscious—especially in extemporaneous stretches of talk—of paragraphing the stream of sound as writers must be when they are writing their manuscript.

The typographical device most commonly used to mark off

paragraphs is indentation. The first line of each new paragraph starts several spaces (usually five or six spaces on the type-writer) from the left-hand margin. Another convention for marking paragraphs in printed texts is the block system: starting every line at the left-hand margin but leaving double or triple spacing between each paragraph.

In this section, only three aspects of the paragraph are treated: unity, coherence, and adequate development. The traditional means of developing the central idea of a paragraph are mentioned in the section on adequate development, but they are not discussed at length as they are in most of the rhetoric texts. But if writers take care of unity, coherence, and adequate development, they will be taking care of the three most persistent and common problems that attend the composition of written paragraphs.

50

Preserve the unity of the paragraph.

Examples of paragraphs lacking unity:

1 The eminence of Samuel Johnson inclines modern scholars to study his thoughts and opinions. His multifarious knowledge intrigued his contemporaries. Although he manifested his interest in the drama by editing Shakespeare, he did not enjoy the theater. He was envious too of his former pupil David Garrick, the greatest actor of the eighteenth century.

2 "The Cradle Song" from the *Songs of Innocence* has internal rhyme. In this poem, the child is quiet and happy. It has a heavenly image, and throughout the poem, the mother sheds tears of joy. It has a persona—that is, one who speaks for the poet—who is naive and innocent. The poem "Infant Sorrow" contrasts with "The

Paragraphing

Cradle Song,'' and this contrast is very distinct. One can see a
screaming and devilish child. The piping is a harsh sound, and
the child, who's against restrictions, is looking back and realizing
that there is no paradise on earth.

3 Dr. Rockwell let his feelings be known on only one subject: the
administration. He felt that the administrative system was outdated.
Abolishing grades, giving the student a voice in administration,
and revamping the curriculum were three steps he felt should
be taken to improve the system. Dr. Rockwell taught in this manner.
In class, a mysterious aura surrounded him. He was ''hip'' to what
was going on, but he preferred to hear the members of the class
rather than himself. He was quiet and somewhat shy. His eyes
caught everything that went on in class. His eyes generated a
feeling of understanding.

The principle governing paragraph unity is that a paragraph
should develop a single topic or thesis, which is often, but
not always, announced in a topic sentence. Every sentence
in the paragraph should contribute in some way to the development of that single idea. If the writer introduces other ideas
into the paragraph, he will violate the unity of the paragraph
and disorient the reader.

In a sense, all three of the sample paragraphs discuss a
single idea or topic: the first one talks about Samuel Johnson;
the second one talks about William Blake's poetry; the third
one talks about a teacher, Dr. Rockwell. But in another sense,
all three paragraphs present a confusing mixture of unrelated
ideas.

The first sentence of the first sample paragraph, which has
the air of being a ''topic sentence,'' talks about what Samuel
Johnson means to modern scholars. Instead of the second
sentence going on to develop that idea, it mentions what Dr.
Johnson meant to his contemporaries. The third sentence talks
about his attitude toward the drama and the theater. The

fourth sentence mentions his envy of his former pupil David Garrick. What we have in this paragraph is four topics. A whole paper or a whole paragraph could be devoted to the development of each of these four topics, but here these four topics are packed into a single paragraph.

We have observed that the second sample paragraph has a certain unity: each sentence is saying something about a poem by William Blake. But notice that the paragraph talks about *two* poems by Blake. Even though the paragraph is about *two* poems, however, we could still detect some unity in the paragraph if we viewed it as developing a contrast between two poems by the same author. But even if we were generous enough to concede that much unity to the paragraph, it would be difficult for us to perceive a unifying theme for the many disparate things said about the two poems.

The third sample paragraph also has a certain unity: each sentence in the paragraph is talking about the teacher, Dr. Rockwell. And there is a tight unity in the first three sentences: each of these sentences talks about Dr. Rockwell's attitude toward the administration. But with the fourth sentence of the paragraph, the writer introduces another and unrelated topic: a description of how Dr. Rockwell conducted himself in the classroom. If the writer had broken up this stretch of prose into two paragraphs, each of the two paragraphs would have had its own unity.

A paragraph will have unity, will have ''oneness,'' if every sentence in the paragraph has an obvious bearing on the development of a single topic. If the writer senses that he has shifted to the discussion of another topic, he should begin another paragraph.

Paragraphing

51

Compose the paragraph so that it reads coherently.

Examples of incoherent paragraphs:

1 The first stanza of "The Echoing Green" does not correspond with any other poem by Blake. The glory of nature's beauty is presented in vivid details. Emotional intensity is the overall effect of the poem. Blake resents the mechanization which has been brought about by the Industrial Revolution. The rhythm of the verses contributes to the meditative mood.

2 The preceding account illustrates all the frustrations that a beginning golfer experiences. The dominant philosophy is that the golfer who looks the best plays the best. He complicates the game by insisting on perfection the first time he sets foot on the course. More time and money are spent on clothes and equipment than on the most important aspect, skill. Winning is the only goal. Where is the idea of recreation? Try playing without a caddy sometime, and see how much exercise you get.

3 After the program has been written, each line is punched onto a card. The deck of cards is known as the "program source deck." The next step is to load the program compiler into the computer. The compiler is a program written in machine language for a particular computer, which reads the source deck and performs a translation of the program language into machine language. The machine language, in the form of instructions, is punched onto cards. This machine-language deck of cards is known as the "object deck." After the object deck has been punched, the programmer is then able to execute his program. The program is run by loading the object deck into the computer. The run of the program marks the end of the second step.

Coherence is that quality which makes it easy for a reader to *follow* a writer's train of thought as it moves from sentence to sentence and from paragraph to paragraph. It facilitates reading because it ensures that the reader will be able to detect the relationships of the parts. It also reflects the clear thinking of the writer because it results from the writer's arrangement of his thoughts in some kind of perceivable order and from his use of those verbal devices that help to stitch thoughts together. In short, as the roots of the Latin word suggest, (co, "together," + *haerēre*, "to stick"), coherence helps the parts of a discourse "stick together."

Here are some ways in which to achieve coherence in a paragraph (not all of these devices, of course, have to be used in every paragraph):

(a) Repeat key words from sentence to sentence or use recognizable synonyms for key words.

(b) Use pronouns for key nouns. (Because a pronoun gets its meaning from the noun to which it refers, it is by its very nature one of those verbal devices that help to stitch sentences together.)

(c) Use demonstrative adjectives, "pointing words" (**this** statement, **that** plan, **these** developments, **those** disasters).

(d) Use conjunctive adverbs, "thought-connecting words" (**however, moreover, also, nevertheless, therefore, thus, subsequently, indeed, then, accordingly**).

(e) Arrange the sequence of sentences in some kind of perceivable order (for instance, a **time order,** as in a narrative of what happened or in an explanation of how to do something; a **space order,** as in the description of a physical object or a scene; a **logical order,** such as cause to effect, effect to cause, general to particular, particular to general, whole to part, familiar to unfamiliar).

The third of the sample paragraphs above attempts to describe computer programming, a process that most readers would find difficult to follow because it is complicated and

Paragraphing

unfamiliar. But the process will be doubly baffling to readers if it is not described coherently. What makes this description of computer programming doubly difficult for the reader to follow is that the writer is doing two things at once: (1) designating the chronological sequence of steps in the process, and (2) defining the technical terms used in the description of the process. It would have been better if the writer had devoted one paragraph to defining such terms as **program source deck, compiler, program language, machine language, object deck.** Then he could have devoted another paragraph exclusively to the description of the process of "running a program"—first you do this, then you do that, after that you do this, etc. As the paragraph is now, the reader gets lost because he is kept bouncing back and forth between definition of the terms and description of the process.

It is more difficult to suggest ways of revising the first two sample paragraphs; they are so incoherent that it is almost impossible to discover what the principal points were that the writers wanted to put across in them. If we could confer with the writers and ask each what the main idea of his paragraph was, we could then advise him about which of the sentences contributed to the development of that idea (and which sentences had to be dropped because they threatened the unity of the paragraph), about the order of the sentences in the paragraph, and about the verbal devices that would help to knit the sentences together.

Coherence is a difficult writing skill to master, but until the writer acquires at least a measure of that skill, he will continue to be frustrated in his efforts to communicate with others on paper. He must learn how to compose paragraphs so that the sequence of thoughts flows smoothly, easily, and logically from sentence to sentence. He must provide those bridges or links that will allow the reader to pass from sentence to sentence without being puzzled about the relationship of what is said in one sentence to what is said in the next sentence. Note how a skillful writer like Thomas Babington Macaulay stitches his sentences together by repeating key words and by using pronouns, connecting words and phrases, and parallel structures:

> It will be seen that we do not consider Bacon's ingenious analysis of the inductive method as a very useful performance. Bacon was not, as we have already said, the inventor of the inductive method. He was not even the person who first analyzed the inductive method correctly, though he undoubtedly analysed it more minutely than any who preceded him. He was not the person who first showed that by the inductive method alone new truth could be discovered. But he was the person who first turned the minds of speculative men, long occupied in verbal disputes, to the discovery of new and useful truth; and by doing so, he at once gave to the inductive method an importance and dignity which had never belonged to it. He was not the maker of that road; he was not the discoverer of that road; he was not the person who first surveyed and mapped that road. But he was the person who first called the public attention to an inexhaustible mine of wealth, which had been utterly neglected and which was accessible by that road alone. By doing so, he caused that road, which had previously been trodden only by peasants and higglers, to be frequented by a higher class of travellers.

52

Paragraphs should be adequately developed.

Examples of inadequately developed paragraphs:

1 Wilfred Owen combines many types of imagery to get his point across. Most of his imagery is either ironic or sentimental.

Paragraphing

2 The young people now growing up in this drug-oriented atmosphere should be made aware of the disadvantages of their indulging in drugs, just as the young people of the previous generation were cautioned about the disadvantages of their engaging in premarital sex. In both cases, responsibility for one's actions is the chief lesson to be taught.

3 The other ways in which these two men differ were that Richard was content with his life, while the Baron was bored with his. Richard was once married, while the Baron was never married but had a son as a result of an affair.

Generally, one- and two-sentence paragraphs are not effective, except for purposes of emphasis, transition, or dialogue. The preceding one-sentence paragraph can be justified on the grounds that the writer wanted to give special emphasis to a principle by setting it aside in a paragraph by itself. Separate paragraphing for emphasis is a graphic device comparable to italicizing (underlining) a word or a phrase in a sentence for emphasis. Set aside in a paragraph by itself, an important idea achieves a prominence that would be missed if the idea were merged with other ideas in the same paragraph. Imagine, for instance, how the impact of the Eight Beatitudes in the Sermon on the Mount would be diminished if they were strung together, one after the other, in a single paragraph.

A one- or two-sentence paragraph can also be used to mark or announce a transition from one major division of a discourse to the next major division. Transitional paragraphs facilitate reading because they orient the reader, reminding him of what has been discussed and alerting him to what is going to be discussed. They are like signposts marking the major stages of a journey. Note how the following two-sentence paragraph helps to orient the reader:

After presenting his Introduction to *Songs of Experience,* William Blake apparently feels that his readers have been sufficiently warned about their earthly predicament. Let us see now how he uses the poems in *Songs of Experience* to illustrate what the people might do to solve their problems.

One of the conventions in printing is that in representing dialogue in a story we should begin a new paragraph every time the speaker changes. A paragraph of dialogue can be one sentence long or ten sentences long (any number of sentences really). A paragraph of dialogue may also consist of only a phrase or a single word:

"It's a beautiful day, isn't it?" Melvin asked.
"Yup," Hank muttered.
"Remember yesterday?"
"Yup."
"I thought it would never stop raining."
"Me too."

Once an exchange like that gets going, the author can dispense with the identifying tags, because the separate paragraphing will mark the shift in speakers.

But except for the purposes of emphasis, transition, or dialogue, a one- or a two-sentence paragraph can rarely be justified. Except for these purposes, a one- or a two-sentence paragraph is almost a contradiction in terms. There can be little if any development in a single sentence. In a two-sentence paragraph, one of the sentences is likely to be the topic sentence; the remaining sentence is hardly enough to develop the topic idea adequately.

Judgment about whether a paragraph is adequately developed is, of course, a relative matter. Because some ideas need more development than others, no one can say absolutely how many sentences a paragraph needs to be satisfactorily developed. But a topic sentence does set at least a general com-

Paragraphing

mitment that a writer must fulfill. When the writer of the first sample paragraph above says, in what is obviously the topic sentence, **Wilfred Owen combines many types of imagery to get his point across,** we have every right to expect that he will specify and discuss several, if not many, types of imagery. But when he develops that topic idea with only one sentence, which is only slightly less general than his first sentence, we can feel quite safe in pronouncing that *this* paragraph is inadequately developed. An obvious way for him to develop the ideas contained in his two sentences is to cite examples, first of ironic imagery, then of sentimental imagery. To flesh out the mere cataloguing of these examples, he could go on to show how these images help the author "get his point across."

Even if the second sample paragraph were a summary paragraph that followed a paragraph (or several paragraphs) in which the writer had discussed the disadvantages of addiction to drugs, the reader could reasonably expect the writer to say something more about the notion presented in his second sentence. What kind of legal or moral responsibilities does an addict have to himself? What kind of responsibilities does he have to his family and to society in general? Once an addict has been "hooked," can he still be held responsible for his actions? What are the consequences, for himself and for society, of his refusing to be responsible for his actions? These questions suggest ways in which the writer might have expanded his thinly developed paragraph.

The writer of the third sample paragraph might have been able to justify his two-sentence paragraph if there were only *two* "other ways" in which Richard Harenger and the Baron Mordiane differed. But if you knew the stories he was discussing (Somerset Maugham's "The Treasure" and Guy de Maupassant's "Douchoux") and if you had seen the differences he discussed later on in the paper, you would realize that there were other, even more significant, differences that he might have mentioned and discussed in this paragraph. The topic sentence commits the writer to developing an extensive contrast between the two characters; by citing only two rather superficial differences, he has clearly not delivered on his commitment.

A topic sentence will suggest how long a paragraph has to be in order to create an impression of being adequately developed. Some sentences commit a writer to more development than others. A sentence like "There was only one way in which Julie could rouse John out of bed in the morning" obviously entails less development than a sentence like "There were several ways in which Julie could rouse John out of bed in the morning." A writer must train himself to look at a topic sentence and see what it commits him to do in the paragraph. Then of course he must have resources at his command so that he can fulfill his commitment. Sometimes he can draw on examples or illustrations to expand his paragraph; sometimes he can develop his topic idea by stating it in a variety of different ways; sometimes he can expand his paragraph by comparison or contrast or by analogy or by an anecdote; or he can trace out the causes or the consequences of what he is talking about. Invention, discovering something to say, is of course the crucial part of the composition process. Thinly developed paragraphs are the result of a writer's not thinking enough about his subject to discover what he already knows about it and what he needs to find out about it in order to develop it. Almost invariably he knows more about the idea stated in a topic sentence than he puts down in a one- or two-sentence paragraph. He must be made aware, or must force himself to become aware, of all that he really knows about the topic idea.

Punctuation

Graphic punctuation, which is the only kind dealt with in this section, is a feature of the written language exclusively. For the written language, it performs the kinds of functions that intonation (pitch, stress, pause, and juncture) performs for the spoken language. Punctuation and intonation can be considered as part of the grammar of a language, because they join with other grammatical devices (word order, inflections, and function words) to help convey meaning. If writers would regard punctuation as an integral—and often indispensable—part of the expressive system of a language, they might cease to think of it as just another nuisance imposed on them by editors and English teachers.

In *Structural Essentials of English* (New York: Harcourt Brace Jovanovich, 1956), Harold Whitehall has neatly summarized the four main functions of graphic punctuation:

☐ **For LINKING parts of sentences and words.**
   semicolon
   colon
   dash
   hyphen (for words only)

Punctuation

☐ **For SEPARATING sentences and parts of sentences.**

period
question mark
exclamation point
comma

☐ **For ENCLOSING parts of sentences.**

pair of commas
pair of dashes
pair of parentheses
pair of brackets
pair of quotation marks

☐ **For INDICATING omissions.**

apostrophe (e.g. **don't, we'll, it's, we've**)
period (e.g. abbreviations, **Mrs., U.S., A. H. Robinson**)
dash (e.g. **John R——, D——n!**)
triple periods (. . . to indicate omitted words in a quotation)

Punctuation is strictly a convention. There is no reason in the nature of things why the mark **?** should be used in English to indicate a question. The Greek language, for instance, uses **;** (what we call a semicolon) to mark questions. Nor is there any reason in the nature of things why the single comma should be a separating device rather than a linking device. Usage has established the distinctive functions of the various marks of punctuation. And although styles of punctuation have changed somewhat from century to century and even from country to country, the conventions of punctuation set forth in the following section are the prevailing conventions in the United States in the second half of the twentieth century. Although publishers of newspapers, magazines, and books often have style manuals that prescribe, for their own editors and writers, a style of punctuation that may differ in some particulars from the prevailing conventions, the writer who

Punctuation

observes the conventions of punctuation set forth in this section can rest assured that he is following the predominant system in the United States.

60

Put a comma in front of the coordinating conjunction that joins the independent clauses of a compound sentence.

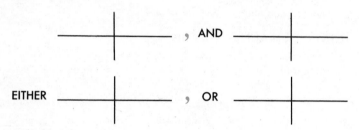

Examples:

1 He disliked this kind of cruel humor, yet when he met the actress at a dinner party, he teased her unmercifully.

2 Alice's embarrassment amused Julian, so he deliberately pursued the conversation with the Dirty Old Man across the aisle.

3 The decision about whether to attend college should be left entirely to the child, and his parents should make every effort to reconcile themselves to his decision.

4 Boswell pointed out several errors in Johnson's biography of Richard Savage, but Johnson probably presented a truer portrait of Savage than all those later biographers who did meticulous research on the minutiae of Savage's life.

5 Either the senators will reject the proposal, or they will modify it in such a way as to make it innocuous.

Pairs of independent clauses joined by one of the coordinating conjunctions (**and, but, or, nor, for, yet, so**) or by one of the correlative conjunctions (**either** . . . **or, neither** . . . **nor, not only** . . . **but**) are the only coordinate pairs that should be separated with a comma (see **62**). The reason why this convention developed is that in many situations, the absence of the comma could lead to an initial misreading of the sentence, as in the second and third examples above or in a sentence like this: "He returned the book for his mother refused to pay anymore fines." In the latter sentence, it would be quite natural for us to read **for** as a preposition. Consequently, we might initially read the sentence this way: **He returned the book for his mother** . . . but when we came to the verb **refused,** we would realize that we had misread the syntax of the sentence and would have to back up and reread the sentence. A comma placed before the coordinating conjunction that joins the two parts of a compound sentence will prevent such misreadings.

Some handbooks authorize you to omit this separating comma if three conditions prevail: (1) if the two clauses of the compound sentence are short, (2) if there is no punctuation within either of the two clauses, and (3) if there is no chance that the syntax will be misread. (The following sentence satisfies these three conditions: "He said he would go and he did.") However, if you *invariably* insert a comma before the coordinating conjunction that joins the independent clauses of a compound sentence, you never have to pause to consider whether there is a chance that your sentence will be misread, and you can be confident that your sentence will always be read correctly the first time.

The safest practice is *always* to insert the comma before the coordinating conjunction that joins the main clauses of a compound sentence.

Punctuation

61

Introductory words, phrases, or clauses should be separated from the main (independent) clause by a comma.

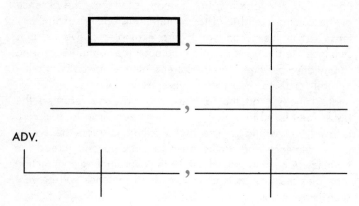

Examples:

1 Underneath, the papers were scorched.
   (*introductory word*)

2 First, one is given the opportunity to select the teachers.
   (*introductory word*)

3 In addition to the logical errors, Doris had made several miscalculations in addition and subtraction.
   (*introductory prepositional phrase*)

4 In all, the dictionaries supply fifteen definitions of the word *grave*.
   (*introductory prepositional phrase*)

5 After hurriedly gathering, the crowd decided to rush the gates.
   (*introductory verbal phrase*)

6 Although he vehemently protested, the violence was not as de-
structive as he predicted it would be.
(*introductory adverbial clause*)

The reason why this convention developed is that the comma
facilitates the reading of the sentence and often prevents an
initial misreading. Without the "protective" comma in the six
examples above, the syntax of those sentences would probably
be misread on the first reading. If the comma were left out,
most readers would probably read the sentences in this way:

1 Underneath the papers . . .
2 [The] first one is given the opportunity . . .
3 In addition to the logical errors [that] Doris had made . . .
4 In all the dictionaries . . .
5 After hurriedly gathering the crowd . . .
6 Although he vehemently protested the violence . . .

The insertion of a comma after the introductory element prevents that kind of misreading.

Even in those instances, however, where there is little or
no chance of an initial misreading, the insertion of a comma
after the introductory word, phrase, or clause will facilitate
the reading of the sentence. Put a comma after the introductory word, phrase, or clause in the following sentences, and
see whether it isn't easier to read the sentences:

Besides the crowd wasn't impressed by his flaming oratory.

Having failed to impress the crowd with his flaming oratory he
tried another tactic.

After he saw that his flaming oratory had not impressed the crowd
he tried another tactic.

If a writer *always* inserts a comma after an introductory
word, phrase, or clause, he will not have to consider each

time whether it would be safe to omit the comma, and he can be confident that his sentence will not be misread.

62

Pairs of words, phrases, or dependent clauses joined by one of the coordinating conjunctions should not be separated with a comma.

Examples:

1 The **mother AND** the **father appeared** in court **AND testified** about their son's activities.

   (*two nouns and two verbs joined by and*)

2 There was nothing they could do **to prevent** the gas attack **OR to protect** themselves against the gas once it had been released.

   (*two infinitive phrases joined by or*)

3 The men **who are able to work BUT who are not willing to work** will not be eligible to receive monthly welfare checks.

   (*two adjective clauses joined by but*)

The principle behind this convention is that what has been joined by one means (the coordinating conjunction) should not then be separated by another means (the comma, a separating device). The function of the coordinating conjunction is to join units of equal rank (e.g. nouns with nouns, verbs with verbs, prepositional phrases with prepositional phrases, participial phrases with participial phrases, adjective clauses with adjective clauses, adverb clauses with adverb clauses). Once pairs of coordinate units have been joined by the conjunction, it makes no sense to separate them with a comma, like this: **the mother, and the father.** If a coordinating conjunction is not used to join the pair, a comma should be used to separate the pair, like this: "the tall, handsome man" (but not "the tall, and handsome man").

The exception to this convention, as in **60**, is a pair of *independent* clauses joined by a coordinating conjunction. According to **60**, a comma should be inserted before the coordinating conjunction, because in this particular structure the omission of the comma could lead—and often does lead—to an initial misreading of the sentence. But there are almost no instances where the use of a comma would prevent the misreading of pairs of words, phrases, or dependent clauses joined by a coordinating conjunction. As a matter of fact, if the first sample sentence were punctuated in this fashion, it would be harder to read: **The mother, and the father appeared in court, and testified about their son's activities.** If some subtle distinction in meaning were effected by these commas, or if the clarity of the sentence were threatened by the absence of the commas, the writer might be able to justify the use of commas in this sentence; but neither of those conditions seems to prevail here. The commas would only confuse the reader.

Unless you have some compelling reason, like protecting the clarity of the sentence, do not separate with a comma pairs of parallel elements that have been joined with a coordinating conjunction.

Punctuation

63

Use a comma to separate a series of coordinate words, phrases, or clauses.

(The parentheses around **and** in the diagrams above indicate that the coordinating conjunction between the last two members of a series may sometimes be dispensed with. For instance, the phrasing **The tall, robust, gray-haired soldier rose to speak** is stylistically preferable to **The tall, robust, and gray-haired soldier rose to speak.**)

Examples:

1 Could he cope with the challenges posed by war, poverty, pollution, and crime?

   (*a series of nouns*)

2 He would have to terminate the war, alleviate the plight of the poor, arrest the contamination of the environment, and hobble the criminal.

   (*series of infinitive phrases, with* **to** *understood in the last three members of the series*)

3 If he is willing to work hard, if he is resourceful enough to formulate sensible policies, if he subordinates his own interests to the interests of the community, he could rescue the nation from the despair that now prevails.

(*series of adverb clauses*)

4 He wanted to save the nation, he knew he could save it, and eventually he did save it.

(*series of independent clauses*)

Whereas the convention stated in **62** says that *pairs* of coordinate words, phrases, or clauses should not be separated with a comma, the convention governing a *series* of coordinate words, phrases, or clauses says that these units should be separated with a comma. (A **series** is to be understood as a sequence of **three or more** coordinate units.) Built on the principle of parallelism (see **27**), the series always involves words, phrases, or clauses of a similar kind. So a series should never couple nouns with adjectives, prepositional phrases with infinitive phrases, adjective clauses with adverb clauses, etc.

The convention that will be recommended here follows this formula: **a, b, and c.** Another acceptable formula for the series is **a, b and c**—where no comma is used between the last two members of the series when they are joined by a coordinating conjunction. The formula **a, b, and c** is adopted here because the alternative formula (**a, b and c**) sometimes leads to ambiguity. Consider the following example, which uses the **a, b and c** formula:

Please send me a gross each of **the red, green, blue, orange and black ties**.

The shipping clerk who received that order might wonder whether five gross of ties (red, green, blue, orange, black) were being ordered or only four gross (red, green, blue, orange-and-black). If five gross were being ordered, a comma after

Punctuation

orange would specify the order unequivocally; if four gross were being ordered, hyphens should have been used to signify the combination of colors.

A more common instance of the ambiguity sometimes created by the use of the **a, b and c** formula is one like the following:

He appealed to **the administrators, the deans and the chairmen.**

In this sentence, it is not clear whether he appealed to three different groups (administrators, deans, chairmen—a meaning that would have been clearly indicated by the **a, b, and c** formula) or to only one group, **administrators,** who are then specified in the double appositive **deans and chairmen.**

Since there is never any chance of ambiguity if you use the **a, b, and c,** you would be well advised to adopt this option for punctuating a series.

64

Nonrestrictive adjective clauses should be enclosed with a pair of commas.

Examples:

1 My oldest brother, **who is a chemist,** was hurt in an accident last week.

2 The shopkeeper caters only to American tourists, **who usually have enough money to buy what they want,** and to aristocratic families.

78

3 Norman Mailer's book, **which most reviewers considered juvenile in its pronouncements,** was severely panned by the women's liberation groups.

A nonrestrictive adjective clause is one that supplies information about the noun that it modifies but information that is not needed to identify the particular person, place, or thing that is being talked about. (The four **that** clauses in the previous sentence, for instance, are **restrictive** adjective clauses—clauses that identify the nouns that they modify.)

In the case of the first example above, the adjective clause **who is a chemist** supplies additional information about **my oldest brother,** but this information is not needed to identify which of the brothers was hurt in the accident, because the adjective **oldest** sufficiently identifies the brother being talked about.

One test to determine whether an adjective clause is nonrestrictive or not is to read the sentence without the adjective clause, and if the particular person, place, or thing being talked about is sufficiently identified by what is left, the adjective clause can be considered nonrestrictive—and, according to the convention, should be marked off with enclosing commas. If, for instance, you were to drop the adjective clause from the first example and say **My oldest brother was hurt in an accident last week,** your readers would not have to ask, "Which one of your brothers was hurt?" The brother is specified by the adjective **oldest,** since there can be only one oldest brother. The clause **who is a chemist** merely supplies some additional but nonessential information about the oldest brother.

Another test to determine whether an adjective clause is nonrestrictive or not is the **intonation** test. Read these two sentences aloud:

Punctuation

He caters to American tourists, who have enough money to buy what they want, and to aristocratic families.

He caters to American tourists who have enough money to buy what they want and to aristocratic families.

In reading the first sentence aloud, native speakers of the language would pause briefly after the words **tourists** and **want** (that is, in the places where the commas are in the written form of the sentence) and would lower the pitch of their voices slightly in enunciating the clause **who have enough money to buy what they want.** In reading the second sentence aloud, native speakers would read right through without a pause and would not lower the pitch of their voices in reading the adjective clause. In writing, it makes a *significant* difference whether the adjective clause in that sentence is or is not enclosed with commas. With the enclosing commas, the sentence means this: He caters to American tourists (who, incidentally, usually have enough money to buy what they want) and to aristocratic families. Without the enclosing commas, the sentence means this: He caters only to those American tourists who have enough money to buy what they want (he doesn't cater to American tourists who don't have enough money to buy) and to aristocratic families. So whether the adjective clause is marked off with commas or not makes a real difference in the *meaning* of the sentence.

There are some instances in which the adjective clause is almost invariably nonrestrictive:

(a) Where the antecedent is a **proper noun,** the adjective clause is usually nonrestrictive:

Martin Chuzzlewit, who is a character in Dickens's novel, . . .

New York City, which has the largest urban population in the United States, . . .

80

The College of William and Mary, which was founded in 1693, . . .

(b) Where, in the nature of things, there could be **only one such** person, place, or thing, the adjective clause is usually nonrestrictive:

My mother, who is now forty-six years old, . . .

Their birthplace, which is Jamestown, . . .

His fingerprints, which are on file in Washington, . . .

(c) Where the identity of the antecedent has been clearly established by the **context,** the adjective clause is usually nonrestrictive:

My brother, who has hazel eyes, . . . (where it is clear from the context that you have only one brother)

The book, which never made the bestseller list, . . . (where the previous sentence has identified the particular book being talked about)

Such revolutions, which never enlist the sympathies of the majority of the people, . . . (where the kinds of revolutions being talked about have been specified in the previous sentences or paragraphs)

Which is the usual relative pronoun that introduces nonrestrictive adjective clauses. **That** is the more common relative pronoun used in restrictive adjective clauses. **Who** (or its inflected forms **whose** and **whom**) is the usual relative pronoun when the antecedent is a person; **that,** however, may also be used when the antecedent is a person and the clause is restrictive: either "the men whom I admire" or "the men that I admire."

65

Restrictive adjective clauses should not be marked off with a pair of commas.

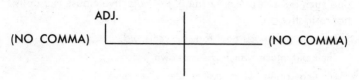

Examples:

1 My brother **who graduated from college in June** was hurt in an accident last week.

2 The poem is about a boy **who has been in Vietnam and has rejoined his family.**

3 The city is obliged to maintain all streets, alleys, and thoroughfares **that are in the public domain.**

A restrictive adjective clause is one that identifies the particular person, place, or thing being talked about. It "restricts" the noun that it modifies; it "defines"—that is, "draws boundaries around"—the noun being talked about.

In the first example above, the adjective clause **who graduated from college in June** is restrictive because it identifies, defines, designates, specifies which one of the brothers was hurt in the accident. Unlike the nonrestrictive adjective clause (see **64**), which merely supplies additional but nonessential information about the noun that it modifies, the restrictive adjective clause supplies information that is needed to identify the noun being talked about.

Whether an adjective clause is restrictive or nonrestrictive makes a substantial difference in the meaning of a sentence. Consider, for instance, these two sentences:

Women who have unusually slow reflexes should be denied a driver's license.

(*restrictive—note the absence of enclosing commas around the* **who** *clause*)

Women, who have unusually slow reflexes, should be denied a driver's license.

(*nonrestrictive—note the enclosing commas around the* **who** *clause*)

The import of the first sentence is that only those women who have unusually slow reflexes should be denied a driver's license. The import of the second sentence is that *all* women should be denied a driver's license, because they have unusually slow reflexes (a claim, incidentally, that is untrue). The presence or absence of commas makes a vital difference in the meaning of the two sentences. For this reason, the punctuation of the sentences is not a matter of option or whim.

If you were speaking those two sentences aloud, your voice would do what the presence or the absence of commas does. In the first sentence, your voice would join the **who** clause with **women** by running through without a pause after **women.** In the second sentence, your voice would pause slightly after **women** and would utter the **who** clause on a slightly lower pitch than the rest of the sentence. In addition to the test of whether the adjective clause is needed to specify the noun referred to, you can use this test of intonation to discriminate restrictive and nonrestrictive clauses.

Restrictive adjective clauses modifying nonhuman nouns should be introduced with the relative pronoun **that** rather than with **which:**

Governments, which are instituted to protect the rights of men, should be responsive to the will of the people.

(*nonrestrictive*)

Punctuation

> Governments that want to remain in favor with their constituents must be responsive to the will of the people.
> (*restrictive*)

Here is another distinctive fact about the phrasing of restrictive and nonrestrictive adjective clauses: the relative pronoun may sometimes be omitted in restrictive clauses, but it may never be omitted in nonrestrictive clauses. Note that it is impossible in English to drop the relative pronouns **who** and **whom** from the following nonrestrictive clauses:

> John, who is my dearest friend, won't drink with me.
> John, whom I love dearly, hardly notices me.

(In the first sentence, however, the clause **who is my dearest friend** could be reduced to an appositive phrase: **John,** *my dearest friend,* **won't drink with me.**)

In restrictive adjective clauses, we sometimes have the option of using or not using the relative pronoun:

> The man whom I love dearly hardly notices me.
> (*with the relative pronoun*)

> The man that I love dearly hardly notices me.
> (*with the relative pronoun*)

> The man I love dearly hardly notices me.
> (*without the relative pronoun*)

In restrictive adjective clauses like these, where the relative pronoun serves as the object of the verb of the adjective clause, the relative pronoun may be omitted. The relative pronoun in restrictive clauses may also be omitted if it serves as the object of a preposition in the adjective clause: "The man I gave the wallet to disappeared" (here the understood **whom** or **that** serves as the object of the preposition **to**).

However, the relative pronoun may *not* be omitted when the relative pronoun serves as the subject of the adjective clause:

He who exalts himself shall be humbled.

(*who* cannot be omitted)

The money that was set aside for scholarships was squandered on roads.

(*that* cannot be omitted)

66

If the independent clauses of a compound sentence are not joined by one of the coordinating conjunctions, they should be joined by a semicolon.

Examples:

1 This refutation is based on an appeal to reason; however, one must remember that an emotional appeal can also move people to reject an argument.

2 All the students spontaneously supported the team; they wanted to show their loyalty, even though they were disappointed with the outcome of the game.

3 He loved his mother; in fact, he practically worshiped her.

Punctuation

The coordinating conjunctions are **and, but, or, nor, for, yet, so.** In the absence of one of those words, the independent clauses of a compound sentence should be spliced together with a punctuation device: the semicolon.

Words and expressions like **however, therefore, then, in fact, indeed, nevertheless, consequently, thus, moreover, on the other hand, on the contrary** are not coordinating conjunctions; they are called conjunctive adverbs. Conjunctive adverbs provide logical links between sentences and between parts of sentences, but they do not function as grammatical splicers. Unlike coordinating conjunctions, which must always be placed *between* the two elements they join, conjunctive adverbs enjoy some freedom of movement in the sentence. In the first sample sentence above, the word **however** is placed between the two independent clauses, but evidence that this conjunctive adverb is not serving as the grammatical splicer of the two clauses is provided by the fact that **however** can be shifted to another position in the sentence: **This refutation is based on an appeal to reason; one must remember, however, that an emotional appeal can also move people to reject an argument.** The coordinating conjunction **but,** on the other hand, could occupy no other position in the sentence than *between* the end of the first clause and the beginning of the next clause.

Nor can the independent clauses of a compound sentence be joined by a comma, because the comma is a separating device, not a joining device. Compound sentences so punctuated are called **comma splices** (see **60**). As indicated in **60**, if a compound sentence is joined by one of the coordinating conjunctions, a comma should be put in front of the conjunction to mark off the end of one independent clause and the beginning of the next independent clause. But when a coordinating conjunction is not present to join the independent clauses, a semicolon must be used to join them. The semicolon serves both to mark the division between the two clauses and to join them.

It is sometimes advisable to use both a semicolon and a coordinating conjunction to join the independent clauses of a compound sentence. When the clauses are unusually long and have commas within them, a semicolon placed before the coordinating conjunction helps to demarcate the end of one clause and the beginning of the next one, as in this example:

> Struggling to salvage what was left of the semester, he pleaded with his English teacher, who was notoriously softhearted, to grant him an extension of time on his written assignments, quizzes, and class reports **;** **but** he forgot that, even with the best of intentions, he had only so many hours every day when he could study and only a limited reserve of energy.

The coordinating conjunction **but** serves to join the two main clauses of the compound sentence, but the use of the semicolon in addition to the conjunction makes it easier to read the sentence.

67

Whenever you use a semicolon, be sure that you have an independent clause on both sides of the semicolon.

Examples of failure to observe this convention:

1 He played the banjo expertly **;** although he couldn't read a note of music.

Punctuation

2 Americans spend far too many hours as spectators of sports instead of as participants in them; watching meaningless drivel on television instead of spending that time reading a book.

3 The two series of poems also differ in style; the *Songs of Experience* being more vague and complex than the *Songs of Innocence*.

This convention is the corollary of **66**. It cautions against using the semicolon to join elements of unequal rank.

In all of the examples above, a semicolon has been used to join units of unequal rank. In all three sentences, there is an independent clause on the *left-hand* side of the semicolon; however, there is no independent clause on the *right-hand* side of the semicolon in any of those sentences.

In the first example above, there is the independent clause **He played the banjo expertly** on the left-hand side of the semicolon, but on the right-hand side of the semicolon, there is only the adverb clause **although he couldn't read a note of music.** That adverb clause belongs with, depends on, the first clause. Since it is an integral part of the first clause, it should be joined with that clause. The effect of the semicolon is to make the adverb clause part of a new clause that begins after the semicolon. But on the right-hand side of the semicolon, there is no independent clause that the subordinate, dependent adverb clause can be a part of.

The first and third examples above can be revised by simply replacing the semicolon with a comma. The second example, however, cannot be revised by a simple change of punctuation. The writer has to supply an independent clause after the semicolon. He can supply that independent clause by adding the words **they spend far too many hours,** so that the whole clause reads, **they spend far too many hours watching meaningless drivel on television instead of spending that time reading a book.** So revised, the sentence has an independent clause on *both* sides of the semicolon.

Like the coordinating conjunction, for which it can serve as a substitute, the semicolon joins parts of equal rank. Therefore, if there is an independent clause on one side of the semicolon, there must be a balancing independent clause on the other side.

68

Use a colon after a grammatically complete lead-in sentence that formally announces a subsequent enumeration, explanation, illustration, or extended quotation.

Examples:

1 The courses I am taking this quarter are as follows: English, sociology, economics, political science, and psychology.

2 His approach works like this: after displaying his product and extolling its virtues, he asks the housewife if she has a small rug that she would like to have cleaned.

3 Examples of the diction used to evoke the horror of the scene include vivid images like these: "coughing like hags," "thick green light," "guttering," "white eyes writhing in his face," "gargling from froth-corrupted lungs."

4 The reaction of the crowd signified only one thing: apathy.

5 (note the use of a colon after a lead-in sentence for an extended quotation in a research paper.)

Toward the end of the *Preface*, Dr. Johnson confessed that he abandoned his earlier expectation that his dictionary would be able to "fix the language":

Punctuation

Those who have been persuaded to think well of my design will require that it should fix our language and put a stop to those alterations which time and chance have hitherto been suffered to make in it without opposition. With this consequence I will confess that I flattered myself for a while; but now begin to fear that I have indulged expectation which neither reason nor experience can justify.

Note that although a word, a phrase, or a clause or a series of words, phrases, or clauses can follow the colon, there must be an independent clause (a grammatically complete sentence) on the left-hand side of the colon.

In accord with this principle, you should not punctuate a sentence in this fashion:

The courses I am taking this quarter are: English, sociology, economics, political science, and psychology.

That punctuation makes no more sense than punctuating a sentence in this way:

My name is: John Adams.

In both cases, the words following the colon are needed to complete the sentence grammatically.

What distinguishes the colon from the dash as a symbolic device is that the colon throws the reader's attention *forward*, whereas the dash as a linking device throws the reader's attention *backward*. What the colon signifies is that what *follows* is a specification of what was formally announced in the clause on the left-hand side of the colon.

69

**Use a dash when the word or word-group that follows
it constitutes a summation, an amplification,
or a reversal of what went before it.**

Examples:

1 English, psychology, history, and philosophy—these were the
courses I took last quarter.

2 If he was pressured, he would become sullen and close-lipped—a
reaction that did not endear him to the president or to the Senate.

3 Time and time again he would admit that his critics were right,
that he should have realized his mistakes, that he should have
read the danger signs more accurately—and then go ahead with
his original plans.

Unlike the colon, which directs the reader's attention forward,
the dash usually directs the reader's attention backward. What
follows the dash, when it is used as a linking device, looks
back to what preceded it for the particulars or details that
spell out its meaning or invest its meaning with pungency or
irony.

The colon and the dash are usually not interchangeable
marks of punctuation. They signal a different relationship between the word-groups that precede them and those that
follow them. After much practice in writing, one develops a
sense for the subtle distinction in relationships that is signaled
by the punctuation in the following sentences:

The reaction of the crowd signified only one thing: apathy.

The crowd clearly indicated their indifference to the provocative
speech—an apathy that later came back to haunt them.

In the first sentence, the lead-in clause before the colon clearly
alerts the reader to expect a specification of what is hinted

Punctuation

at in that clause. In the second sentence, there is no such alerting of the reader in the lead-in clause; but following the dash, there is an unexpected commentary on what was said in the lead-in clause, a summary commentary that forces the reader to look backward. The colon and the single dash are both linking devices, but they signal different kinds of thought relationships between parts of the sentence.

Finally, the writer should be cautioned to avoid using the dash as a catchall mark of punctuation, one that indiscriminately substitutes for periods, commas, semicolons, etc.

70

Use a pair of dashes to enclose abrupt parenthetical elements that occur within a sentence.

—— —— (enclosing dashes)

Examples:

1 In some instances—although no one will admit it—the police over-reacted to the provocation.

2 What surprised everyone when the measure came to a vote was the chairman's reluctance—indeed, downright refusal—to allow any riders to be attached to the bill.

3 One of them—let me call him Jim Prude—is clean-shaven and dresses like an Ivy Leaguer of the early 1950s.

4 The new campus—or cluster of campuses—was built on a hill overlooking a gently rolling valley.

The three devices used to set off parenthetical elements in written prose are commas, parentheses, and dashes. The kind of parenthetical element that should be enclosed with a pair of dashes is the kind that interrupts the normal syntactical flow of the sentence. What characterizes such elements in the examples above is that they abruptly arrest the normal flow of the sentence to add some qualifying or rectifying information. The rhetorical effect of the enclosing dashes is to give the parenthetical element an unusual measure of emphasis.

A pair of parentheses is another typographical device used to mark off parenthetical elements in a sentence. Enclosure within parentheses is used mainly for those elements that merely add information or identification, as in sentences like these:

> All the companies that used the service were charged a small fee (usually $500) and were required to sign a contract (an "exclusive-use" agreement).

> The manager of each franchise is expected to report monthly to NARM (National Association of Retail Merchants) and to "rotate" (take turns doing various jobs) every two weeks.

The typographical device used to set off the mildest kind of interrupting element is a pair of commas. Whether to enclose a parenthetical element with commas or with parentheses or with dashes is more a matter of stylistic choice than a matter of grammatical necessity. There are degrees of interruption and emphasis, and with practice, a writer develops an instinct for knowing when to mark off parenthetical elements with commas (lowest degree of interruption and emphasis), when to mark off with parentheses (middle degree), and when to mark off with dashes (highest degree). Consider the degrees of interruption and emphasis in the following sentences:

> That agency, as we have since learned, reported the incident directly to the Department of Justice.

> During the postwar years (at least from 1946 to 1952), no one in the agency dared challenge a directive from higher up.

> When the order was challenged, the attorney general—some claim it was his wife—put a call through to the president.

Punctuation

A dash is made on the typewriter with two unspaced hyphens and with no space before the dash or after the dash. (In handwriting, the dash should be made slightly longer than a hyphen.)

Example:

> He forgot—if he ever knew—the functions of the various marks of punctuation.

Do not hit the spacebar on the typewriter *before* the first hyphen, *between* the first and second hyphen, or *after* the second hyphen. In short, do not hit the spacebar at all in forming the dash on the typewriter.

Avoid the following kinds of typography in forming the dash on the typewriter:

He forgot–if he ever knew–the functions of the
various marks of punctuation.

He forgot – if he ever knew – the functions of the
various marks of punctuation.

He forgot –– if he ever knew –– the functions of
the various marks of punctuation.

He forgot – – if he ever knew – – the functions of
the various marks of punctuation.

Mechanics

The graphic devices dealt with in this section might be, and often are, classified as punctuation. But because such graphic devices as italics, capitalization, and numbers are not correlated—as punctuation marks are—with the intonational patterns of the spoken language, these devices are grouped in a separate section under the heading Mechanics. In the spoken language, a word printed with a capital letter is pronounced no differently from the same word printed with a lower-case letter. Nor is the italicized title of a book pronounced any differently from that same title printed without italics. (Italics used for emphasizing a word or phrase, however, do correspond to stress in the spoken language.) Even quotation marks, which one might regard as correlated with the spoken language, do not correspond to anything the voice does when it quotes direct speech.

But whether one classifies these graphic devices as punctuation or as mechanics is immaterial. What is important to remember is that these devices are part of the written language exclusively and that they facilitate the reading of that language. Most readers would have at least momentary difficulty making sense of the following string of words:

> candy cane replied in the united states people use gas to refer to the liquid propellant that is called petrol in other english speaking countries

If the proper punctuation and mechanics were used with that string of words, readers would be spared the momentary difficulty:

> Candy Cane replied, "In the United States, people use *gas* to refer to the liquid propellant that is called *petrol* in other English-speaking countries."

Deprived of the resources that the human voice has to clarify the meaning of a spoken utterance, the writer should be eager to use all those typographical devices that make it easier for his readers to grasp what he is trying to convey in the written medium.

80

The closing quotation mark always goes outside the period or the comma.

,"   ."

Examples:

1 The author announces at the beginning of his article that he is going to cite only "facts."

2 "I know," she said, "that you are telling me a barefaced lie."

3 Mrs. Robinson's "bearded, sandaled, unwashed hippies," many of whom had traveled over a thousand miles to the festival, represented an aggregation of straight-A students.

81 Quotation Mark, Colon and Semicolon

This is a clear case where usage, rather than logic, has established the prevailing convention. Many reputable British printers put the closing quotation mark *inside* the period or the comma, especially when the quotation marks enclose something less than a complete sentence—e.g. a word or phrase or dependent clause. But American printers almost universally put the closing quotation mark *outside* the period or the comma.

The advantage of such consistency is that you never have to pause and ask yourself, "Is this a case where the quotation mark goes inside or outside the period?" Whether it is a single word or a phrase or a dependent clause or an independent clause that is enclosed, the closing quotation mark always goes *outside* the period or the comma; or, to put the emphasis another way, the comma and the period always go *inside* the closing quotation mark.

In handwriting, take care to put the quotation mark *outside* the period or comma, not on *top* of it, like this: ';' '.' In the case of quotations within quotations, both the single-stroke quotation mark and the double-stroke quotation go *outside* the period or the comma, as in this example:

"I read recently," he said, "that Patrick Henry never said 'Give me liberty or give me death."

81

The closing quotation mark always goes inside the colon or the semicolon.

"; ":

Mechanics

Examples:

1 He called this schedule of activities his "load": work, study, exercise, recreation, and sleep.

2 He told his taunters, "I refuse to budge"; his knees, however, were shaking even as he said those words.

Whereas the closing quotation mark always goes *outside* the period or the comma, it always goes *inside* the colon or the semicolon. If a writer has occasion to use quotation marks with a colon or a semicolon, he has only to recall that the convention governing the placement of the closing quotation mark in relation to these is just the opposite of the convention for the period and the comma.

82

The closing quotation mark sometimes goes inside the question mark and sometimes goes outside the question mark.

?"   "?

Examples:

1 Who was it that said, "I regret that I have but one life to lose for my country"?

2 He asked her bluntly, "Will you marry me?"

3 When will they stop asking, "Who then is responsible for the war?"

Although the closing quotation mark always goes outside a period or a comma and always goes inside a colon or a semicolon, you have to consider each case particularly before deciding whether to put the closing quotation inside or outside the question mark. Fortunately, the criteria for determining whether the quotation mark goes inside or outside are fairly simple to apply:

(a) When the whole sentence, but not the unit enclosed in quotation marks, is a question, the question mark goes *outside* the closing quotation mark. (See the first example above.)

(b) When only the unit enclosed in quotation marks is a question, the question mark goes *inside* the closing quotation mark. (See the second example above.)

(c) When the whole sentence and the unit enclosed in quotation marks are both questions, the question mark goes *inside* the closing quotation mark. (See the third example above.)

In all cases, the question mark serves as the terminal punctuation for the entire sentence. In the case of (*b*), you do not add a period outside the closing quotation mark, and in the case of (c), you do not add another question mark outside the closing quotation mark.

83

The titles of books, newspapers, magazines, professional journals, plays, long poems, movies, operas, works of art, and ships should be italicized by underlining.

Examples:

1 The critics have always rated Hemingway's *A Farewell to Arms* above his *For Whom the Bell Tolls*.

(*titles of books*)

Mechanics

2 He has already published three articles in the *Quarterly Journal of Speech.*

(*title of a professional journal*)

3 To support his contention, he quoted a passage from an anonymous article in *Newsweek.*

(*title of a magazine*)

4 The moonship *Falcon* settled down about 400 yards from the projected landing site.

(*title of the* Apollo 15 *"ship"*)

Printers use a special italic type, which slants slightly to the right, to set off certain words in a sentence from other words that are printed in regular roman type (upright letters). In handwriting or typewriting, one italicizes words by <u>underlining</u> them.

Although italics are used with the titles of all of the items listed above, the writer most often has occasion to use italics with the titles of book-length or pamphlet-length published materials. Besides being a convention, the use of italics for titles can also protect meaning in some instances. If someone wrote "I didn't really like Huckleberry Finn," a reader might be uncertain (unless the context gave him a clue) whether the writer was revealing his dislike for Mark Twain's novel or for the character of that name in the novel. If the writer intended to indicate that he disliked the novel, he could transmit that message unambiguously by simply underlining (italicizing) the proper name.

How does one decide whether a poem is long enough to have its title italicized? As with most relative matters, the extreme cases are easily determinable. Obviously, a sonnet would not qualify as a long poem, but Milton's *Paradise Lost* would. It is the middle-length poem that causes indecision. A reliable rule of thumb is this: if the poem was ever published as a separate book or if it could conceivably be published as a separate book, it could be considered long enough to be set forth in italics. According to that guideline, T. S. Eliot's *The Wasteland* would be considered a long poem, but his "The Love Song of J. Alfred Prufrock" would be considered a short poem and therefore should be enclosed in quotation marks (see **84**). But if you cannot decide whether a poem is "long" or "short," either italicize the title or enclose it in quotation marks and use that system consistently throughout the paper.

84

The titles of articles, essays, short stories, short poems, and chapters of books should be enclosed in quotation marks.

Examples:

1 Thomas Gray's "Elegy Written in a Country Churchyard" is reputed to be the most anthologized poem in the English language.
(title of a short poem)

2 Hollis Alpert's "Movies Are Better Than the Stage" first appeared in the *Saturday Review of Literature*.
(title of an article in a periodical)

3 J. F. Power's "The Valiant Woman" was reprinted in 1947 in *The Prince of Darkness and Other Stories*.
(title of a short story in a collection of stories.)

The general rule here is that the titles of published material that is *part* of a book or a periodical should be enclosed in quotation marks.

Mechanics

That general rule, however, needs some qualification. If you were referring to an excerpt from a long work, you should not enclose the title of that long work in quotation marks; you should italicize the title of the long work, even though the excerpt was part of a collection or anthology.

Example:
Only Book III of Wordsworth's *The Prelude* is included in our anthology.

(not "The Prelude"—*even though only part of the long work is reprinted in the book*)

The title of a paper that you write should not be enclosed in quotation marks, nor should it be italicized—unless your title is itself a quotation or unless it contains elements that are normally italicized or enclosed in quotation marks.

The right and the wrong format of a title for a paper submitted for a class assignment or for publication:

WRONG: "The Evolution of Courtly Love in Medieval Literature"

The Evolution of Courtly Love in Medieval Literature

RIGHT: The Evolution of Courtly Love in Medieval Literature

The Evolution of Courtly Love in Chaucer's Troilus and Criseyde

Courtly Love in Herrick's "Corinna's Going a-Maying" and Marvell's "To His Coy Mistress"

The Shift in Meaning of the Word Love in Renaissance Lyrics

"One Giant Step for Mankind"—Historic Words for a Historic Occasion

85

Italicize (underline) words referred to as words.

Examples of references to words as words:

1 He questioned the appropriateness of *honesty* in this context.
2 *The American Heritage Dictionary* defines *dudgeon* as "a sullen, angry, or indignant humor."
3 Unquestionably, *trudged* is a more specific verb than *walked*.

"He questioned the appropriateness of honesty in this context."
"He questioned the appropriateness of *honesty* in this context."
Although composed of the same words in the same order, those two sentences carry different meanings. The first sentence signifies that what is being challenged is the appropriateness of the thing (the abstract quality) designated by the word *honesty;* the second sentence signifies that what is being questioned is the appropriateness of the word itself. It is the italics alone that indicate to the reader the difference in meaning between these two sentences.

Italics (underlining) are a graphic device commonly used to distinguish a word being used *as a word* from that same word used as a symbol for an idea. (In handwritten or typewritten copy, you italicize words by <u>underlining</u> them.) An alternative but less common device for marking words used as words is to enclose the words in quotation marks, as in this example:

The heavy use of such sensory diction as "juicy," "empurpled," "smooth," "creaked," "murmuring" helps to evoke the scene and make it almost palpable to the reader.

Since both devices are authorized by convention, the writer should adopt one system and use it consistently. The use of italics is probably the safer of the two systems, however,

Mechanics

because quotation marks are also used to enclose quoted words and phrases, as in the sentence, We heard her say "yes." (Here *yes* is not being referred to as a word but is a quotation of what she said.)

86

Italicize (underline) foreign words and phrases, unless they have become naturalized or Anglicized.

Examples of foreign words and phrases:

1 Why does the advertiser, whose mouthpiece is the copywriter, allow himself to be presented before the public as a poet **malgré lui?**

2 The advice to begin a short story as close to the climax as possible is a heritage of Horace's advice to begin a narrative **in medias res** rather than **ab ovo.**

3 There had been a remarkable revival in the late 1960s of the **Weltschmerz** that characterized the poetry of the Romantics.

So that the reader will not be even momentarily mystified by the sudden intrusion of strange-looking words into a stream of English words, printers use italics to underscore foreign words and phrases. The graphic device of italics does not ensure, of course, that the reader will be able to translate the foreign locution, but it does prevent confusion by alerting the reader to the presence of non-English words.

Some foreign words and phrases, like habeas corpus, divorcee, mania, siesta, subpoena, have been used so often in an English context that they have been accepted into the vocabulary as "naturalized" English words and therefore as not needing to be set forth in italics. All unabridged desk dictionaries have a system for indicating which foreign words and phrases have become naturalized and which have *not* become naturalized. Since dictionaries sometimes differ in their judgments about the naturalized status of certain foreign expressions, the writer should consistently follow the dictates of the dictionary available to him in determining whether a word or phrase needs italics.

An obvious exception to the rule is that proper nouns designating foreign persons, places, and institutions, even when they retain their native spelling and pronunciation, are *always* set forth without italics (underlining).

87

Compound words should be hyphenated.

Examples of compound words:

1 Because I had the normal six-year-old's "sweet tooth," I was irresistibly lured by the candy store.

2 He was attracted to anti-Establishment movements because they lacked policy-making administrators.

3 They scheduled the examinations in three-quarter-hour segments.

4 He preferred eighteenth-century literature because of its urbanity.

English reveals its Germanic origins in its tendency to form compounds—that is, to take two or more existent words and join them together to create a single unit that designates a thing or a concept quite different from what the individual words designate. A familiar example is the word **basketball.** When the two distinct words **basket** and **ball** were first joined to designate an athletic game or the kind of ball used in that game, the words were linked by a hyphen: **basket-ball.** When repeated use had made this new compound familiar to readers,

Mechanics

the hyphen was dropped, and the two words were printed as a single word with no break between the two constituent parts.

Dozens of words in English have made this transition from a hyphenated compound to a single amalgamated word (e.g. *postoffice, skyscraper, briefcase, airport*). But hundreds of compounds are still printed with a hyphen, either because they have not been used enough to achieve status as unmarked hybrids or because the absence of a hyphen would lead to ambiguity. A reliable dictionary will indicate which compounds have made the passage and which have not.

With the exception of those words that have become recognized amalgams, a hyphen should be used to link

(a) two or more words functioning as a single grammatical unit.

his **never-say-die** attitude (adjective)

the junkyard had a huge **car-crusher** (noun)

the hoodlums **pistol-whipped** him (verb)

he conceded the point **willy-nilly** (adverb)

(b) two-word numbers (from 21 to 99) when they are written out.

twenty-one, thirty-six, forty-eight, ninety-nine

(c) combinations with prefixes **ex-** and **self-**.

ex-chairman, ex-wife, self-denial, self-contradictory

(d) combinations with prefixes like **anti-, pro-, pre-, post-,** when the second element in the combinations begins with a capital letter or a number.

anti-Establishment, pro-American, pre-1929, post-1945

(e) combinations with prefixes like **anti-, pro-, pre-, re-, semi-, sub-, over-,** when the second element begins with the letter that occurs at the end of the prefix.

anti-intellectual, pro-oxidant, pre-election, re-entry, semi-independent, sub-basement, over-refined

(f) combinations where the unhyphenated compound might be mistaken for another word.

re-cover (the chair)
recover (the lost wallet)

re-sign (the contract)
resign (his office)

co-op
coop

With these exceptions, compounds formed with these prefixes now tend to be written as a single word (e.g. *antiknock, preconscious, prodemocratic, postgraduate*). And at least one authority would have all the compounds in (e), above, spelled solid. As against this, other authorities make distinctions that allow for *preelection* and *reentry* while prohibiting *antiintellectual*. In adopting any system that makes such distinctions, the writer should consistently follow the conventions of the authority consulted.

Frequently in writing, only a hyphen will clarify ambiguous syntax. If the writer of the third sample sentence had not used hyphens **(They scheduled the examinations in three quarter hour segments),** the reader would not be able to determine whether the examination was divided into three fifteen-minute segments (a meaning that would be clearly signaled by this placement of the hyphen: **three quarter-hour segments**) or whether it was divided into forty-five-minute segments (a meaning that is clearly signaled by this placement of hyphens:

Mechanics

three-quarter-hour segments). There is a similar ambiguity in the sentence "He was the only new car dealer in town." A speaker would be able to clarify the ambiguous syntax of that sentence by the appropriate intonation of the voice. But in writing, only a hyphen will make clear whether the writer meant to say **He was the only new car-dealer in town** or **He was the only new-car dealer in town.**

88

A word can be broken and hyphenated at the end of a line only at a syllable-break; a one-syllable word can never be broken and hyphenated.

For the writer, two valuable bits of information are supplied by the initial entry of every word in the dictionary: (1) the spelling of the word, and (2) the syllabification of the word. The word **belligerent,** for instance, is entered this way in the dictionary: **bel·lig·er·ent.** If that word occurred at the end of a line and you saw that you could not get the whole word in the remaining space, you could break the word and hyphenate it at any of the syllables marked with a raised period. But you could not break the word in any of the following places: **bell-igerent, belli-gerent, bellige-rent.**

Since the syllabification of English words is often unpredictable, it is safest to consult a dictionary when you are in doubt about where syllable-breaks occur. But after a while, you learn certain "tricks" about syllabification that save you a trip to the dictionary. A word can usually be broken

(a) after a prefix (**con-, ad-, pre-, un-, im-**).
(b) before a suffix (**-tion, -ment, -less, -ous, -ing**).

(c) between double consonants (**oc-cur-rence, cop-per, prig-gish**).

One-syllable words, however, can never be divided and hyphenated, no matter how long they are. So if you come to the end of a line and find that you do not have enough space to squeeze in single-syllable words like *horde, grieve, stopped, quaint, strength, wrenched,* leave the space blank and write the whole word on the next line. You have no choice.

Even in the interest of preserving a right-hand margin, you should not divide a word so that only one or two letters of it stand at the end of the line or at the beginning of the next line. Faced with divisions like *a-bout, o-cean, un-healthy, grass-y, dioram-a, flor-id, smok-er, live-ly,* you should put the whole word on that line or the next one. Remember that the hyphen itself takes up one space.

89

Never begin a sentence with an Arabic number; spell out the number or recast the sentence.

Examples of sentences beginning with numbers:

1 Five hundred and twenty-two men reported to the induction center.

   NOT: 522 men reported to the induction center.

2 Nineteen hundred and fifty-five was a very good year.

   OR: Most people agree that 1955 was a very good year.
   NOT: 1955 was a very good year.

3 Eight million two hundred thousand dollars was appropriated by Congress for arms.

   OR: Congress appropriated $8.2 million for arms.
   NOT: $8,200,000 was appropriated by Congress for arms.

Mechanics

The reason why this convention developed is that an Arabic number looks strange when it stands at the beginning of a sentence. There is, too, the convention that we always capitalize the first letter of every new sentence, and there is no way of capitalizing an Arabic number.

Observing this convention will undoubtedly work a hardship on the writer who has to report many statistics in discursive prose. Faced with that assignment, the writer could plead with whoever commissioned the report that a chart or graph would be a more appropriate medium.

Format of the Research Paper

General Instructions

A research paper reports the results of some investigation, experiment, interview, or reading that you have done. Some of the ordinary papers you write are also based on personal investigations, interviews, and reading, and when they are based on external sources, you should acknowledge those sources in the text of your paper. For instance, you can reveal the source of information or quotations by saying in the text "Mr. Stanley Smith, the director of the Upward Bound project, with whom I talked last week, confirmed the rumor that . . ." or "James Reston said in his column in last Sunday's *New York Times* that . . ." Authors of research papers also use identifying lead-ins like those in the text, but in addition they supply, in footnotes, any further bibliographical information (for instance, the exact date of the newspaper you are quoting from and the number of the page on which the passage occurred) that readers would need if they wanted to check the sources. By revealing this specific information about the source, the author enables his readers to check whether he has been accurate or fair in his reporting, and he also enhances his credibility.

Format of the Research Paper

In the pages that follow, we will present some advice about gathering and reporting material from outside sources, some models for footnote and bibliography forms, and some sample pages from a research paper. The instructor or the journal for whom you write may prescribe a format that differs from the advice given here, but if no specific instructions are given, you can follow these suggestions and models with the assurance that they conform to the prevailing conventions for research papers.

(a) GATHERING NOTES

Each person eventually discovers a system of gathering notes that works best for him. Some people, for instance, just scribble their notes on full sheets of paper or in spiral notebooks. The system that works best for most researchers, however, is to record notes and quotations on 3 x 5 or 4 x 6 cards—one note or quotation to a card. The advantage of having your notes on cards is that later you can select and arrange the cards to suit the order in which you are going to use them in your paper. It is considerably more difficult to select and arrange notes if they are written out, one after the other, on full sheets of paper.

(b) SELF-CONTAINED NOTECARDS

Each notecard should be self-contained—that is, it should contain all the information you would need to document that material properly if you used it in your paper. A notecard is self-contained if you never have to go back to the original source to recover any bit of information about the note. So each notecard should carry at least this much information:

1. The card should carry some indication whether the note is paraphrased or quoted verbatim. Don't trust your memory to be able to distinguish later whether a note is paraphrased or quoted.

2. If quoted material covers more than one page in the source from which it was copied, you should devise some system of indicating just where the quoted material went over to the next page. If later you use only part of that quotation, you have to know whether to cite one page (p. 189) or two pages (pp. 189–90) in the footnote. Some notation like (→ p. 190) inserted in the notecard after the last word on the page (in this case, after the last word on p. 189) in the original source will help you determine later whether you need to cite one page or two pages.

3. The notecard should contain all the bibliographical information needed to document the note in a footnote of your paper: name of the author, title of the book or article, publication information, and page numbers (see Model Footnotes). If you are taking several notes from the same source, you can devise some shorthand system so that you do not have to write out all the bibliographical information on every notecard.

(c) **WHAT NEEDS TO BE FOOTNOTED?**

You will have to develop a sense for what needs to be documented with a footnote. Here are some guidelines to help you:

1. Ordinarily, every direct quotation should carry a footnote. However, if you were doing a research paper on, say, a novel, you could be spared having to document every quotation from the novel by using a footnote like this the *first time* you quote from the novel:

Format of the Research Paper

> John Steinbeck, The Grapes of Wrath (New
> York: Viking Press, 1939), p. 134. Hereafter
> all quotations from this first edition of the
> novel will be documented with a page number in
> parentheses immediately after the quotation.

2. Paraphrased material may or may not need a footnote. If the fact or information that you report in your own words is *generally known* by people knowledgeable on the subject, you probably would not have to document that paraphrased material. For instance, if you were writing a research paper on the assassination of Abraham Lincoln, you probably would not have to document your statement that John Wilkes Booth shot Lincoln in Ford's Theater in Washington in April of 1865, because that historical fact is common knowledge. But if one of the arguments in your paper concerned the *exact time of the day* when he was shot, you would have to document your statement that Lincoln was shot at 8:40 p.m. on the evening of April 14, 1865. When, however, you cannot resolve your doubt about whether paraphrased material needs to be documented with a footnote that reveals the source of the information, document it.

3. When you are summarizing, in your own words, a great deal of information that you have gathered from your reading, you can be spared having to document several sentences in that summary by putting a footnote number after the *first sentence* of the summary and using a footnote like this:

[10]For the biographical information presented in this and the subsequent paragraph,
I am indebted to Minnie M. Brashear, <u>Mark
Twain</u>: <u>Son</u> <u>of</u> <u>Missouri</u> (Chapel Hill: University of North Carolina Press, 1934), pp. 34–65
and Gamaliel Bradford, "Mark Twain," <u>Atlantic
Monthly</u>, 125 (April, 1920), 462–73.

(d) KEEP QUOTATIONS TO A MINIMUM

A research paper should not be just a pastiche of long quotations stitched together by an occasional comment or by a
transitional sentence by the author of the paper. You should
use your own words as much as possible, and when you do
quote, you should keep the quotation brief. Often a quoted
phrase or sentence will make a point more emphatically than
a long quotation. You must learn to look for the phrase or
sentence that represents the kernel of the quotation and to
use that extract rather than the full quotation. Otherwise, the
point you want to make with the quotation may be lost in all
the verbiage. You will be more likely to keep your quotations
short if you try to work most of the quotations into the frame-
work of your own sentence, like this:

Frank Ellis calls such an interpretation "the
biographical fallacy, the assumption that an
exact, one-to-one correspondence exists between the person who is imagined to be speaking the lines of the poem (the Spokesman) and
the historical personage who is known to have
written the poem."[12]

Format of the Research Paper

Sometimes, however, when you find it difficult to present the essential point in a short extract, you will have to quote something at greater length. Long quotations (two sentences or more) should be *inset* from the left-hand margin and *single-spaced*, with *no quotation marks enclosing the quotation*, like this:

Frank Ellis offers this cogent argument to refute the charge that the Epitaph is not integrated with the rest of the poem:

> The evidence for this is said to lie in the fact that there are disparities between the two accounts that are given of the Stonecutter, one by the aged Swain and the other in Epitaph. But it has never been pointed out that these disparities are deliberate and dramatic. The illiterate old rustic is unsympathetic. His disapproval has been softened no doubt by death, but it is still apparent that to him the Stonecutter seemed lazy, queer, unsociable, and probably crazy. But the Epitaph enables the reader to see around this characterization. For the Spokesman, who composed the Epitaph, is an outlander, a fellow poeta ignotus, and therefore unsympathetic.[15]

(e) USE A LEAD-IN FOR ALL QUOTATIONS

Every direct quotation should be accompanied by a lead-in phrase or clause, which at least identifies by name the person who is about to speak. But it further aids coherence if the lead-in also points up the pertinence of the subsequent quotation to what you have been talking about or to what you are going to talk about. Here are some typical identifying and orienting lead-ins:

Edmund Wilson countered this charge by saying that "there is never any reason for supposing that anybody but the governess sees the ghosts."

"It apparently did not occur to any of Wilson's critics," says Oscar Cargill in defense of Wilson's interpretation, "that James might have an adequate motive for disguising his purpose in the tale."

Robert Heilman has this to say about Wilson's interpretation of Henry James's haunting story:

(following this last lead-in would be either a single sentence enclosed in quotation marks or a series of sentences inset and single-spaced, like the extended quotation in (d) above)

(f) THE FORMAT OF FOOTNOTES

The first line of every footnote is indented from the left-hand margin (usually the same number of spaces as paragraph indentations in the body of the paper), but any subsequent lines of the same footnote are brought out to the left-hand margin. If footnotes are put at the bottom of the page, they are single-spaced *within* the footnote and double-spaced *be-*

Format of the Research Paper

tween footnotes. If footnotes are put on separate pages, they are double-spaced both *within* the footnote and *between* footnotes. See Model Footnotes and Sample Pages for further information about the format of footnotes.

(g) PRIMARY AND SECONDARY FOOTNOTES

Primary footnote forms (that is, those giving full bibliographical information) must be used the *first time* a source is cited. Thereafter, that same source can be documented with a secondary footnote form (that is, a shortened form). See Model Footnotes and Sample Pages for the format of primary and secondary footnotes.

(h) THE FORMAT OF BIBLIOGRAPHY ENTRIES

Bibliography entries are arranged alphabetically on separate pages at the end of the research paper. The list of entries is alphabetized according to the last name of the author (or in the case of unsigned articles, according to the first significant word in the title). For that reason, the names of authors are inverted in the Bibliography—e.g. **Heilman, Robert.** The first line of each bibliography entry begins at the left-hand margin, and any subsequent lines in that entry are indented (just the opposite of the format of footnotes). Bibliography entries are single-spaced *within* the entry and double-spaced *between* entries. (If, however, the paper is being submitted for publication, the bibliography entries are double-spaced both within the entry and between entries.) See Bibliography Forms and Sample Bibliography Page for other differences between the format of footnotes and the format of bibliography entries.

ELLIPSIS PERIODS

Ellipsis periods (three spaced periods) are used to indicate that words or whole sentences have been omitted from a direct quotation:

```
The President said last week that "the Ameri-
can people . . . would not tolerate such vio-
lence."
```

(*note that there is a space between periods; wrong form:* **...**)

```
Philip Gove said in a letter to the New York
Times:

   The paragraph is, of course, a monstrosity,
   totally removed from possible occurrence in
   connection with any genuine attempt to use
   words in normally expected context. . . . A
   similar artificial monstrosity could be con-
   trived by jumbling together inappropriate
   words from formal literary language or from
   the Second Edition.
```

(*the fourth period in this instance is the period used to mark the end of the sentence. Because of this period and the capital letter with which the next group of words begins, we know that at least one sentence was omitted from what Mr. Gove said*)

Usually there is no need to put ellipsis periods at the beginning or end of a quotation, because the reader knows that the quotation has been extracted from a larger context. Reserve ellipsis periods for indicating omissions *within* quotations.

Format of the Research Paper

(i) SQUARE BRACKETS

Square brackets are used to enclose anything that the author of the research paper inserts into a direct quotation from another author:

About this tendency to indulge in scatological language, H. A. Taine wrote, "He [Swift] drags poetry not only through the mud, but into the filth; he rolls in it like a raging madman, he enthrones himself in it, and bespatters all passers-by."

The Senator was emphatic in stating his reaction to the measure: "This action by HEW [Health, Education, and Welfare] will definitely not reverse the downward spiral [of prices and wages] that has plagued us for the last eight months."

We find this entry in the Japanese admiral's diary: "Promptly at 8:32 on Sunday morning of December 6 [sic], 1941, I dispatched the first wave of bombers for the raid on Perl Harber [sic]."

(the *sic* is a Latin adverb, meaning "thus," "in this manner," and is used to let the reader know that the error in logic or fact or grammar or spelling in the quotation has been copied exactly as it was in the original source. It is italicized because it is a foreign word)

If your typewriter does not have keys that make square brackets, you will have to draw the brackets with a pen after you remove the paper from the typewriter.

Format of the Research Paper:
Model Footnotes

The models for footnotes and for bibliography follow the forms prescribed in *The MLA Style Sheet,* 2nd ed. (New York: Modern Language Association, 1970), one of the most widely used systems in America.

The models here are single-spaced within the footnote and double-spaced between footnotes, as they would be if they appeared at the bottom of the page in a research paper or a dissertation. For the double-spacing of footnotes, see the Model for Footnotes Entered on Separate Pages on p. (147).

For the bibliography form for each of these model footnotes, see the next section (p. 129).

Primary Footnotes

(the first reference to a source)

(1) A single book by a single author:

```
   Victor Perlo, The Negro in Southern Agricul-
ture (New York: International Publishers, 1953),
p. 103.
```

> Ronald R. Nelson, <u>The</u> <u>Home</u> <u>Office</u>, <u>1782-1801</u> (Durham, N.C.: Duke Univ. Press, 1969), pp. 75-6.

(Notice that the first line of the footnote is indented and that subsequent lines of the footnote start at the left-hand margin. The p. is the abbreviation of page; pp. is the abbreviation of pages.)

(2) A single book by more than one author:

> Paul A. Baran and Paul M. Sweezy, <u>Monopoly</u> <u>Capital</u> (New York: Monthly Review Press, 1966), p. 392.

(3) A book of more than one volume:

> William Lee Hays and Robert L. Winkler, <u>Sta-</u> <u>tistics</u>: <u>Probability</u>, <u>Inference</u>, <u>and</u> <u>Decision</u> (New York: Holt, Rinehart, and Winston, 1970), II, 137.

(Whenever a volume number is cited [here the Roman numeral II], the abbreviation p. or pp. is not used in front of the page number.)

(4) A book edited by one or more editors:

> <u>Essays</u> <u>in</u> <u>American</u> <u>Economic</u> <u>History</u>, ed. Alfred W. Coats and Ross M. Robertson (London: Edward Arnold, 1969), pp. 268-9.

Format of the Research Paper

> The Letters of Jonathan Swift to Charles Ford, ed. David Nichol Smith (Oxford: Clarendon Press, 1935), p. 187.

(Here the abbreviation **ed.** stands for **edited by.**)

(5) An essay or a chapter by an author in an edited collection:

> Martin J. Svaglic, "Classical Rhetoric and Victorian Prose," The Art of Victorian Prose, ed. George Levine and William Madden (New York: Oxford Univ. Press, 1968), pp. 268–70.

(6) A new edition of a book:

> Oswald Doughty, A Victorian Romantic, Dante Gabriel Rossetti, 2nd ed. (London: Oxford Univ. Press, 1960), p. 35.

(Here the abbreviation **ed.** stands for **edition.**)

(7) A book that is part of a series:

> William Heytesbury, Medieval Logic and the Rise of Mathematical Physics. University of Wisconsin Publications in Medieval Science, No. 3 (Madison: Univ. of Wisconsin Press, 1956), p. 97.

(Here the abbreviation **No.** stands for **Number.**)

(8) A book in a paperback series:

> Edmund Wilson, <u>To</u> <u>the</u> <u>Finland</u> <u>Station</u>.
> Anchor Books (Garden City, N.Y.: Doubleday,
> 1955), p. 130.

(9) A translation:

> Fyodor Dostoevsky, <u>Crime</u> <u>and</u> <u>Punishment</u>,
> trans. Constance Garnett (New York: Heritage
> Press, 1938), p. 351.

> Jacques Ellul, <u>A</u> <u>Critique</u> <u>of</u> <u>the</u> <u>New</u>
> <u>Commonplaces</u>, trans. Helen Weaver (New York:
> Knopf, 1968), pp. 139–40.

(10) A signed and an unsigned article from an encyclopedia:

> J. A. Ewing, "Steam–Engine and Other Heat–
> Engines," <u>Encyclopaedia</u> <u>Britannica</u>, 9th ed.
> XXII, 475–7.

> "Dwarfed Trees," <u>Encyclopedia</u> <u>Americana</u>,
> 1948, IX, 445.

(Since encyclopedias periodically undergo revision and updating, the particular edition consulted should be indicated by a date or a number. In the bibliography, unsigned articles are filed alphabetically according to the first significant word in the title—here Dwarfed.)

(11) An article from a journal:

> Nelson Adkins, "Emerson and the Bardic Tra-
> dition," <u>PMLA</u>, 72 (1948), 665.

Format of the Research Paper

> Theodore Otto Windt, Jr., "The Diatribe:
> Last Resort for Protest," <u>QJS</u>, 58 (1972), 9–10.

(*Well-known scholarly journals are commonly referred to by their abbreviated titles. Here PMLA stands for Publications of the Modern Language Association; QJS stands for Quarterly Journal of Speech. Volume numbers of journals are now designated by an Arabic number [here 72 and 58] rather than, as formerly, by a Roman numeral. Because the volume number has been cited, the abbreviations p. and pp. are not used in front of the page numbers.*)

(12) An article in a popular magazine:

> Robert J. Levin, "Sex, Morality, and
> Society," <u>Saturday</u> Review, 9 July 1966, p. 29.

> Charles E. Silberman, "Technology Is Knock-
> ing on the Schoolhouse Door," <u>Fortune</u>, Aug.
> 1966, pp. 121–2.

(*Note that Saturday Review is a weekly magazine; Fortune is a monthly. Because no volume number is cited, p. and pp. are used in front of the page numbers.*)

(13) A signed and an unsigned article in a newspaper:

> Art Gilman, "Altering U.S. Flag for Politi-
> cal Causes Stirs a Legal Debate" <u>Wall</u> <u>Street</u>
> <u>Journal</u>, 12 June 1970, p. 1.

> "Twin Games Bid: Wrestling, Judo," <u>New</u> <u>York</u>
> <u>Times</u>, 9 April 1972, Section 5, p. 15, cols. 4–6.

(*For editions of a newspaper with multiple sections, each with*

Model Footnotes

its own pagination, it is necessary to cite the section in addition
to the page number. It is helpful also to give column numbers.
Sometimes, if an article appeared in one edition of a newspaper but not in other editions, it is necessary to specify the
particular edition of the newspaper—e.g. New York Times, *Late
City Ed.*, 4 Feb. 1972, p. 12, col. 1.)

(14) A signed book review:

John F. Dalbor, rev. of Meaning and Mind: A
Study in the Psychology of Language, by Robert
F. Terwilliger, Philosophy & Rhetoric, 5 (1972),
60–1.

Brendan Gill, rev. of Ibsen, by Michael
Meyer, New Yorker, 8 April 1972, p. 128.

(The first review appeared in a scholarly journal; the second
review appeared in a weekly magazine. The abbreviation **rev.**
stands for **review.**)

Secondary Footnotes

(shortened forms after a source has once been given in full)

15Nelson, p. 80.

(This is the shortened form of the second footnote given in
(1) under Primary Footnotes.)

16Hays and Winkler, II, 140.

(This is the shortened form of the footnote given in (3) under
Primary Footnotes.)

127

Format of the Research Paper

[17]Ibid., I, 87.

(**Ibid.** *is the abbreviation of the Latin adverb* **ibidem,** *meaning "in the same place." Ibid. may be used if the source in that footnote is the same as the one cited in the immediately preceding footnote. However, if a reader would have to turn back one or more pages to find the last source cited, it would be better to use the last-name shortened form: Hays and Winkler, I, 87. There must be added to Ibid. only what changes from the previous source. Thus in footnote 17 above, I and 87 were added to Ibid. because both the volume number and the page number changed from the previous footnote. If only the page number changed, footnote 17 would read thus: Ibid., p. 145. If nothing changed, footnote 17 would read thus: Ibid.)*

[18]Wilson, Finland Station, pp. 220–2.

(*When more than one book or article by the same author has been cited in a paper, you must use an abbreviated title in addition to the surname of the author in order to identify the source. In footnote 18 above, Finland Station is an abbreviated form of the full title To the Finland Station.)*

[19]"Rendezvous with Ecology," p. 97.

(*In the case of an anonymous article or book, the title or a shortened form of it has to be used in subsequent references to that source.)*

Format of the Research Paper:
Models for Bibliography

The form of a bibliography entry differs in some ways from that of a footnote reference. The following shows how the two forms handle a citation for the same book.

BIBLIOGRAPHY	FOOTNOTE
Ryan, Edwin. <u>A College Handbook to Newman</u>. Washington, D.C.: Catholic Education Press, 1930.	Edwin Ryan, <u>A College Handbook to Newman</u> (Washington, D.C.: Catholic Education Press, 1930), p. 109.

The first line begins at the left-hand margin, with all subsequent lines indented.

The first line is indented, with all subsequent lines brought out to the left-hand margin.

Format of the Research Paper

BIBLIOGRAPHY	FOOTNOTE
The name of the author is inverted (last name first) for purposes of alphabetizing the list of entries.	The name of the author is set down in the normal order.
The three main divisions of author, title, and publishing data are separated by periods.	The three main divisions of author, title, and publishing data are separated by commas.
Place of publication, name of the publisher, and publication date comprise a separate sentence following the title.	Place of publication, name of the publisher, and publication date are enclosed in parentheses as part of the single sentence making up the entry.
The subtitle, if any, should be included in the citation. See (2) below.	The subtitle, if any, may be omitted in the citation.
There is no page reference unless the entry is for an article or part of a collection, in which case the full span of pages (first page and last page) is cited.	Only a specific page reference is cited.

Corresponding Bibliography Forms for the Fourteen Model Footnotes

(If the research paper is submitted as an assignment in a course, the bibliography entries may be single-spaced within the entry and double-spaced between entries, as in the Model for a Bibliography Page (p. 150). If, however, the paper is being submitted to a journal for possible publication, the entries should be double-spaced both within the entry and between the entries, as they are in these models.)

(1) A single book by a single author:

```
Perlo, Victor. The Negro in Southern Agricul-
    ture. New York: International Publishers,
    1953.

Nelson, Ronald R. The Home Office, 1782-1801.
    Durham, N.C.: Duke Univ. Press, 1969.
```

(2) A single book by more than one author:

```
Baran, Paul A., and Paul M. Sweezy. Monopoly
    Capital: An Essay on American Economic and
    Social Order. New York: Monthly Review
    Press, 1966.
```

(Only the name of the first author should be inverted. Notice that the subtitle, which was omitted in the footnote, is included here.)

Format of the Research Paper

(3) A book of more than one volume:

Hays, William Lee, and Robert L. Winkler.
   Statistics: _Probability_, _Inference_, _and_
   Decision. 2 vols. New York: Holt, Rinehart,
   and Winston, 1970.

(4) A book edited by one or more editors:

Essays _in_ _American_ _Economic_ _History_. Ed.
   Alfred W. Coats and Ross M. Robertson. London: Edward Arnold, 1969.

The _Letters_ _of_ _Jonathan_ _Swift_ _to_ _Charles_ _Ford_.
   Ed. David Nichol Smith. Oxford: Clarendon
   Press, 1935.

(In the bibliography, these books would be filed alphabetically according to the first significant word in the title—
Essays and **Letters** respectively.)

(5) An essay or a chapter by an author in an edited collection:

Svaglic, Martin J. "Classical Rhetoric and
   Victorian Prose." _The_ _Art_ _of_ _Victorian_
   Prose. Ed. George Levine and William Madden.
   New York: Oxford Univ. Press, 1968, pp.
   268-88.

(Because this essay is part of a collection, the full span of pages is cited in the bibliography.)

(6) A new edition of a book:

Doughty, Oswald. <u>A</u> <u>Victorian</u> <u>Romantic</u>, <u>Dante</u>
   <u>Gabriel</u> <u>Rossetti</u>. 2nd ed. London: Oxford
   Univ. Press, 1960.

(7) A book that is part of a series:

Heytesbury, William. <u>Medieval</u> <u>Logic</u> <u>and</u> <u>the</u>
   <u>Rise</u> <u>of</u> <u>Mathematical</u> <u>Physics</u>. University of
   Wisconsin Publications in Medieval Science,
   No. 3. Madison: Univ. of Wisconsin Press,
   1956.

(8) A book in a paperback series:

Wilson, Edmund. <u>To</u> <u>the</u> <u>Finland</u> <u>Station</u>. Anchor
   Books. Garden City, N.Y.: Doubleday, 1955.

(9) A translation:

Dostoevsky, Fyodor. <u>Crime</u> <u>and</u> <u>Punishment</u>.
   Trans. Constance Garnett. New York: Heritage
   Press, 1938.

Format of the Research Paper

Ellul, Jacques. _A_ _Critique_ _of_ _the_ _New_ _Common-_
    places. Trans. Helen Weaver. New York:
    Knopf, 1968.

(10) A signed and an unsigned article from an
encyclopedia:

Ewing, J. A. "Steam—Engine and Other Heat—
    Engines." _Encylopaedia_ _Britannica_. 9th ed.,
    XXII, 473—526.

"Dwarfed Trees." _Encyclopedia_ _Americana_. 1948,
    IX, 445—6.

(Notice that the full span of pages of these articles is given.)

(11) An article from a journal:

Adkins, Nelson. "Emerson and the Bardic Tradi-
    tion." _Publications_ _of_ _the_ _Modern_ _Language_
    Association, 72 (1948), 662—7.

Windt, Theodore Otto, Jr. "The Diatribe: Last
    Resort for Protest." _Quarterly_ _Journal_ _of_
    Speech, 58 (1972), 1—14.

(Although in footnotes well-known scholarly journals are commonly referred to by their abbreviated title, it is advisable to give the full title in the bibliography.)

(12) An article in a popular magazine:

Levin, Robert J. "Sex, Morality, and Society."
Saturday Review, 9 July 1966, pp. 29–30.

Silberman, Charles E. "Technology Is Knocking
on the Schoolhouse Door." Fortune, Aug.
1966, pp. 120–25.

(13) A signed and an unsigned article in a newspaper:

Gilman, Art. "Altering U. S. Flag for Political Causes Stirs a Legal Debate." Wall
Street Journal, 12 June 1970, p. 1.

"Twin Games Bid: Wrestling, Judo." New York
Times, 9 April 1972, Section 5, p. 15,
cols. 4–6.

(14) A signed book review:

Dalbor, John B. Review of Meaning and Mind: A
Study in the Psychology of Language, by

Format of the Research Paper

 Robert F. Terwilliger. <u>Philosophy</u> & <u>Rhe-</u>
  <u>toric</u>, 5 (1972), 60–61.

Gill, Brendan. Review of <u>Ibsen</u>, by Michael
 Meyer. <u>New</u> <u>Yorker</u>, 8 April 1972, pp. 126–30.

Format of the Research Paper:
Model Research Paper (with footnotes
at bottom of page)

THE CONTROVERSY ABOUT THE EPITAPH

IN THOMAS GRAY'S "ELEGY WRITTEN IN A

COUNTRY CHURCHYARD"

by

Kevin Krewmeister

English 535
Dr. Morgan
April 15, 1973

The Controversy About the Epitaph in Thomas Gray's "Elegy Written in a Country Churchyard"

Since its first publication in a quarto edition by Robert Dodsley in 1751, Thomas Gray's "Elegy Written in a Country Churchyard" has become one of the best-known and most-anthologized poems in the English language. Generations of schoolboys have been required to memorize the poem, and even today one finds older people who are prompted to recite the poem at the mere mention of the title. Even those who never bothered to memorize the poem are amazed to find verses like the following echoing in their head:

The short and simple annals of the poor.

The paths of glory lead but to the grave.

Full many a flower is born to blush unseen,
And waste its sweetness on the desert air.

> He gave to Mis'ry all he had, a tear,
> He gain'd from Heav'n (t'was all he wish'd)
> a friend.[1]

Even those readers whose taste does not run to the kind of sententious verse that Gray's poem represents concur with Dr. Johnson's judgment of the poem: "Had Gray written often thus it had been vain to blame, and useless to praise him."[2]

This widely known and apparently simple poem, however, has elicited a great deal of critical commentary in recent years. In addition to elaborate explications of the poem,

[1]All my quotations from the "Elegy" are taken from the final approved version of 1753, as printed in Herbert W. Starr and John R. Hendrickson, eds., The Complete Poems of Thomas Gray, English, Latin, and Greek (Oxford: Clarendon Press, 1966). Hereafter, quotations from this edition will be documented by line numbers in parentheses.

[2]Samuel Johnson, "Gray," The Lives of the English Poets, ed. George Birkbeck Hill (Oxford: Clarendon Press, 1905), III, 442.

there has been a series of articles dealing
with the knotty problem presented by the Epitaph, the final three quatrains of the poem.
Who was the "Youth to Fortune and to Fame Unknown" mentioned in the Epitaph? Is it the
spokesman of the poem, the "me" of line 4? Or
is it the village stonecutter, the "unletter'd
muse" mentioned in line 81? Or is it Richard
West, Gray's close friend, whose death in 1742
may have prompted Gray to write the poem? Or
is it Gray himself? The question of who the
Youth is does not admit of an easy answer,
largely because of the ambiguities of reference in stanzas 24-29 of the poem. In this
paper, I propose to examine a number of
twentieth-century interpretations of the Epitaph and then indicate which interpretation
strikes me as being the most persuasive.

The controversy with which I am dealing in

this paper was initiated in 1923 by Odell

Shephard's article.[3] Shephard begins his pur-

suit of the question about who the Youth men-

tioned in the Epitaph is by considering the

candidates most often proposed by readers of

the poem: "(a) a purely imaginary personifica-

tion of the type poeta; (b) an actual poet en-

tirely unknown to fame, an Ignotus, whom Gray,

however, had known at Stoke Poges or else-

where; (c) Thomas Gray himself."[4] On pp.

345–352, Shephard considers each of these pro-

posed candidates in turn and presents his rea-

sons for rejecting all of them. Having re-

jected these candidates, he is then faced with

the obligation to propose his own candidate

and to argue the plausibility of his proposal.

[3]"A Youth to Fortune and to Fame Unknown,"
Modern Philology, 20 (1923), 347–73.

[4]Ibid., p. 348.

It is interesting to observe the kind of evidence that Professor Shephard uses and the skill with which he manipulates fact, conjecture, and inference to build his case. He bases his interpretation on the three manuscript versions of the "Elegy": the Eton MS., the Pembroke MS., and the Wharton MS.[5] The earliest version of the poem, which was entitled "Stanzas wrote in a Country Church-yard," ended with line 72. The latest version, the one eventually published, added a new ending, which introduced the "Youth to Fortune and to Fame unknown" and his Epitaph. After a careful examination of the various versions of the

[5] A detailed description of the various manuscript versions is given in Francis G. Stokes, ed., An Elegy Written in a Country Churchyard (Oxford: Clarendon Press, 1929), pp. 23-6. Herbert W. Starr has also presented an illuminating study of the successive versions of the poem in his article "Gray's Craftsmanship," JEGP, 45 (1946), 415-29.

poem, Shephard conjectures that "at some time prior to June, 1750, Gray had among his papers two independent poems in the _Elegy_ stanza: the epitaph, addressed to some person as yet unknown to us, and a poem in twenty-two stanzas about a country churchyard which ended with a clear reference to the poet himself."[6] Seeing a similarity in theme and tone between those two poems, Gray saw that by supplying a bridge, he could unite the two poems. According to Shephard's hypothesis, stanzas 19-29 serve as that bridge.

Having erected that hypothesis, Shephard must now find a plausible candidate for the Youth referred to in the Epitaph. After reviewing the circumstances of Gray's life at the time and his relations with his friends,

[6]Shephard, p. 366.

Shephard proposes Richard West as the Youth of the Epitaph. In the following paragraph, Professor Shephard summarizes his arguments in support of his claim that Richard West is the likeliest candidate for the Youth of the Epitaph:

Clearly, the character and history of Richard West fit closely into the description and epitaph of the Youth to Fortune and to Fame Unknown. He was Gray's dearest friend. He was a solitary, "crazed with care," and a poet. His real promise was cut short by an early death. Fair Science certainly did not frown upon him, for he was said by Bryant, a school fellow of both, to have been more learned than Gray. Although his birth was not humble--he was a grandson of Bishop Burnet and son of a vice-chancellor of Ireland--neither was it noble. . . . The person commemorated in the Epitaph is characterized by a line very similar to one in which West had characterized himself. We have seen the difficulties into which the view that the Youth stands for Gray necessarily leads. There is nothing in the description and Epitaph which does not harmonize with the theory that the Youth stands for Richard West.[7]

[7]Shephard, pp. 371-2.

So persuasive was the argument that Professor
Shephard built for his hypothesis that I left
his article believing that the question about
the identity of the Youth had been settled
once and for all and that Gray's poem was in
the tradition of other English elegies of personal bereavement, like Milton's "Lycidas" and
Arnold's "Thyrsis." But I had not yet read the
equally persuasive cases that other critics
had made for their candidates. The knot was to
become tighter, not looser.

In 1949, Herbert W. Starr published an article in which he took issue with Shephard's
assumption that the Epitaph was originally a
separately composed poem commemorating Richard
West and maintained that West could not be accepted as the Youth of the Epitaph until other
possible candidates had been more decisively
eliminated from consideration than Shephard

had managed to do in his article.[8] Starr
raised the very telling point that nowhere in
any of the extant manuscripts of the poem was
there any evidence that the Epitaph ever existed independently of the rest of the poem.
Although Starr agreed with Shephard that the
Ignotus, some unknown poet, could safely be
disregarded as the Youth of the Epitaph, he
was not so willing to concede Shephard's dis-
missal of the _Poeta_ or of Gray himself as candidates.[9]

[8]"'A Youth to Fortune and to Fame Unknown':
A re-estimation," _JEGP_, 48 (1949), 97-107.

[9]Ibid., pp. 99-101.

Format of the Research Paper:
Model for Footnotes Entered on Separate Pages

(If footnotes are entered on separate pages at the end of a research paper submitted as a classroom assignment, they may be single-spaced within the footnote and double-spaced between footnotes, just as they are at the bottom of the page in the sample pages of the research paper. If a paper is submitted for publication, however, the footnotes must be entered on separate pages and must be double-spaced both within and between footnotes, as they are in the model below.)

[1] All my quotations from the "Elegy" are taken from the final approved version of 1753, as printed in Herbert W. Starr and John R. Hendrickson, eds., The Complete Poems of Thomas Gray, English, Latin, and Greek (Oxford: Clarendon Press, 1966). Hereafter, quotations from this edition of the poem will be documented by line numbers in parentheses.

Format of the Research Paper

²Samuel Johnson, "Gray," The Lives of the English Poets, ed. George Birkbeck Hill (Oxford: Clarendon Press, 1905), III, 442.

³Odell Shephard, "A Youth to Fortune and to Fame Unknown," Modern Philology, 20 (1923), 347-73.

⁴Ibid., p. 348.

⁵A detailed description of the various manuscript versions is given in Francis G. Stokes, ed., An Elegy Written in a Country Churchyard (Oxford: Clarendon Press, 1929), pp. 23-6. Herbert W. Starr has also presented an illuminating study of the successive versions of the poem in his article "Gray's Craftsmanship," JEGP, 45 (1946), 415-29.

⁶Shephard, p. 366.

⁷Ibid., pp. 371-2.

⁸H. W. Starr, "'A Youth to Fortune and to Fame Unknown': A Re-estimation," JEGP, 48 (1949), 97-107.

148

Model for Footnotes Entered on Separate Pages

[9]Ibid., pp. 99–101.

[10]Frank H. Ellis, "Gray's _Elegy_: The Biographical Problem in Literary Criticism,"
PMLA, 66 (1951), 984.

[11]Starr, "Gray's Craftsmanship," p. 420.

[12]Ellis, pp. 987–8.

[13]John H. Sutherland, "The Stonecutter in
Gray's 'Elegy,'" _Modern Philology_, 55 (1957),
12.

Format of the Research Paper:
Model For a Bibliography Page

(The bibliography for a paper submitted as a classroom assignment may be single-spaced, as it is in the model below. The bibliography for a paper submitted for publication, however, should be double-spaced, both within the entry and between entries, as in the Models for Bibliography. Notice that the entries below are arranged in alphabetical order.)

                    BIBLIOGRAPHY

Ellis, Frank H. "Gray's _Elegy_: The Bio-
    graphical Problem in Literary Criticism."
    _Publications of the Modern Language Associ-
    ation_, 66 (1951), 971–1008.

Johnson, Samuel. "Gray." _The Lives of the Eng-
    lish Poets_. Ed. George Birbeck Hill. Ox-
    ford: Clarendon Press, 1905, III, 421–42.

Ketton-Cramer, Robert W. _Thomas Gray: A Biog-
    raphy_. Cambridge, Eng.: Cambridge Univ.
    Press, 1955.

Model for Bibliography Page

Martin, Roger. <u>Chronologie</u> <u>de</u> <u>la</u> <u>Vie</u> <u>et</u> <u>de</u>
<u>l'Oeuvre</u> <u>de</u> <u>Thomas</u> <u>Gray</u>. Paris: Les Presses
Universitaires, 1931.

Shephard, Odell. "A Youth to Fortune and to
Fame Unknown." <u>Modern</u> <u>Philology</u>, 20 (1923),
347-73.

Starr, Herbert W., and John R. Hendrickson,
eds. <u>The</u> <u>Complete</u> <u>Poems</u> <u>of</u> <u>Thomas</u> <u>Gray</u>, <u>Eng</u>-
<u>lish</u>, <u>Latin</u>, <u>and</u> <u>Greek</u>. Oxford: Clarendon
Press, 1966.

Starr, Herbert W. "Gray's Craftsmanship."
<u>Journal</u> <u>of</u> <u>English</u> <u>and</u> <u>Germanic</u> <u>Philology</u>,
45 (1946), 415-29.

_____. "'A Youth to Fortune and to
Fame Unknown': A Re-estimation." <u>Journal</u> <u>of</u>
<u>English</u> <u>and</u> <u>Germanic</u> <u>Philology</u>, 48 (1949),
97-107.

Stokes, Francis G., ed. <u>An</u> <u>Elegy</u> <u>Written</u> <u>in</u> <u>a</u>
<u>Country</u> <u>Churchyard</u>. Oxford: Clarendon Press,
1929.

Sutherland, John H. "The Stonecutter in Gray's
'Elegy.'" <u>Modern</u> <u>Philology</u>, 55 (1957),
11-3.

Toynbee, Paget, and Leonard Whibley, eds. <u>The</u>
<u>Correspondence</u> <u>of</u> <u>Thomas</u> <u>Gray</u>. 3 vols. Ox-
ford: Clarendon Press, 1935.

Forms For Letters

General Instructions

The one type of writing that most people engage in after they leave school is letter-writing. They will almost certainly write letters to parents, friends, and acquaintances; occasionally they may feel compelled to write a letter to the editor of a newspaper or magazine; and sometimes they may write more formal letters to institutions or officials for such purposes as applying for a job, requesting information or service, or seeking redress of some grievance. Although they do not have to be much concerned about the niceties of form when they are writing to intimate friends, they would be well advised to observe the conventions of form and etiquette in letters to people with whom they are not familiar enough to address them by their first name.

Letters written to acquaintances are commonly referred to as "familiar letters." Although "anything goes" in letters to acquaintances, one should keep in mind that even the most intimate acquaintance is flattered if the author of the letter observes certain amenities of form. A model for a familiar letter appears on p. 156. Here is a list of the conventions for the familiar letter:

General Instructions

(a) Familiar letters may be written on lined or unlined paper of any size, but usually they are written on note-size stationery of some pastel color.

(b) Familiar letters may be handwritten and may be written on both sides of the page.

(c) The writer puts his own address and the date at the right-hand side of the heading but does not, as in a business letter, put the name and address of the person to whom he is writing at the left-hand side of the heading.

(d) Depending on the degree of intimacy with the addressee, the writer can use salutations like these: **Dear Mom, Dear Bill, Dear Elizabeth, Dear Mrs. Connolly.** The salutation is usually followed by a comma rather than the more formal colon.

(e) The body of the letter may be written in indented paragraphs, single- or double-spaced.

(f) Depending on the degree of intimacy with the addressee, the writer may use complimentary closes like these: **Much love, Affectionately, As ever, Cordially, Fondly.**

(g) Depending on the degree of intimacy with the addressee, the writer may sign his full name or just his first name or nickname.

Formal letters addressed to organizations or strangers or superiors are commonly called "business letters." The form of business letters is more strictly prescribed than that of familiar letters. A model for a business letter appears on p. 157. Here is a list of the conventions for the business letter:

(a) Business letters are written on $8\frac{1}{2}$ x 11 unlined paper or on $8\frac{1}{2}$ x 11 paper with a printed letterhead.

(b) Business letters must be typewritten, on one side of the page only.

Forms for Letters

(c) If the writer is using paper with a printed letterhead, he needs to type only the date below the letterhead, either in the center of the page or flush with the right-hand margin. If he is using blank paper, he should type in, flush with the right-hand margin and in single-spaced block form, his address and the date.

(d) Flush with left-hand margin and in single-spaced block form, the writer should type the name and address of the person or the organization to whom he is writing. (This is the same form that will be used in addressing the envelope.)

(e) Two spaces below this inside address and flush with the lefthand margin, the writer should type the salutation, followed by a colon. If the writer is addressing an organization rather than a specific person in that organization, he can use salutations like **Dear Sir** or **Gentlemen** or **Dear Madam** or **Ladies.** If the writer knows the name of the person, he should use **Mr.** or **Miss** or **Mrs.** or, if uncertain about the marital status of a woman, **Ms.,** followed by the last name: **Dear Mr. Abernathy, Dear Miss Sentnor, Dear Mrs. Allen, Dear Ms. Yellen.** Women who feel that marital status should be no more specified in their own case than in that of a man (for whom **Mr.** serves, irrespective of whether he is married) prefer **Ms.** to **Mrs.** or **Miss. Messrs.** is the plural of **Mr.; Mmes.** is the plural of **Miss** or **Mrs.** Professional titles may also be used in the salutation: **Dear Professor Winslow, Dear Dr. Morgan.** (*Webster's Seventh New Collegiate Dictionary,* on pp. 1173–76, carries a list of the forms of address to various dignitaries [judges, clergymen, bishops, congressmen, etc.].)

(f) The body of the letter should be single-spaced, except for double-spacing between paragraphs. Paragraphs are not indented but start flush with the left-hand margin.

(g) The usual complimentary closes for business letters are

these: **Yours truly, Very truly yours, Sincerely, Sincerely yours.** The complimentary close is followed by a comma.

(h) The writer should type his name about three or four spaces below the complimentary close. He should not preface his name with his professional title (e.g. **Dr., Rev.**) nor follow it with his degrees (e.g. **M.A., Ph.D.**), but below his typed name he may indicate his official capacity (e.g. **President, Director of Personnel, Managing Editor**). The writer should sign his name in the space left between the complimentary close and his typed name.

(i) If one or more copies of the letter are being sent to someone, that fact should be indicated with a notation like this in the lower left-hand side of the page (**c.** is the abbreviation of **copy; cc.** is the abbreviation of **copies**):

c. Mary Hunter

cc. Mary Hunter
    Robert Allison

(j) If the letter was dictated to, and typed by, a secretary, that fact should be indicated by a notation like this, flush with the left-hand margin and below the writer's signature (the writer's initials are given in capital letters, and the secretary's are given in lower-case letters): WLT/cs or WLT:cs.

See the following models for a Familiar Letter and a Business Letter

Sample Handwritten Familiar Letter

1410 17th avenue
Columbus, Ohio 43214
June 10, 1973

Dear Jim,

Bob and I decided to leave for Washington on Friday, June 16, at 4: a.m. We figured that we would save time if you met us at the Brandywine exit Ramp (Exit 58) of I-70. Get your brother to drive you there by 4:45.

Al decided at the last minute not to go, because he starts his job on Monday, and since jobs are hard to find this summer, it wouldn't be too bright to pass this one up. My sister Jane sends her love.

Write if you get hung up and can't meet us.

Sincerely,
Tom

P.S. Bring your gasmask.

Sample Typescript Business Letter

239 Riverside Road
Columbus, Ohio 43210
March 30, 1973

Mr. Thomas J. Weiss
Manager, Survey Division
Acme Engineering Company, Inc.
5868 Fanshawe Drive
Omaha, Nebraska 68131

Dear Mr. Weiss:

Mr. Robert Miller, sales representative of the
Rushmore Caterpillar Company of Columbus and a
long-time friend of my father, told me that
when he saw you at a convention in Chicago recently, you indicated you would have two or
three temporary positions open this summer in
your division. Mr. Miller kindly offered to
write you about me, but he urged me to write
also.

By June I will have completed my junior year
in the department of Civil Engineering at Ohio
State University. Not only do I need to work
this summer to finance my final year of college, but I also need to get some practical
experience in surveying on a large road-build-
ing project such as your company is now
engaged in. After checking with several of
the highway contractors in this area, I have
learned that all of them have already hired
their quota of engineering students for the
summer.

For the last three summers I have worked for the Worley Building Contractors of Columbus as a carpenter's helper and as a cement-finisher. Mr. Albert Michael, my foreman for the last three summers, has indicated that he would write a letter of reference for me, if you wanted one. He understands why I want to get some experience in surveying this summer, but he told me that I would have priority for a summertime job with Worley if I wanted it.

Among my instructors in civil engineering, the two men who know me best are Dr. Theodore Sloan, who says that he knows you, and Mr. A. M. Slater. Currently I have a 3.2 quality-point average in all my subjects, but I have straight A's in all my engineering courses. For the last two quarters I have worked as a lab assistant for Professor Sloan.

I am anxious to get experience in my future profession and I am quite willing to relocate for the summer. I own a 1969 Volkswagen that I could use to commute several miles each day to the job site, if that is necessary. I am in good health, and I am willing to work very hard. If you want any letters of recommendation from any of the men named in my letter, please let me know, but perhaps you will be satisfied by Mr. Miller's testimony about me.

Sincerely yours,

Oscar Jerman

Oscar Jerman

c. Robert Miller

158

**Forms for Letters:
Models for Addressing
Envelopes (reduced size)**

FAMILIAR LETTER

Thomas O'Conner
1410 17th Ave.
Columbus, Ohio 43214

Mr. James Faran
430 Marion Manoz Dr.
Newark, Ohio 43055

BUSINESS LETTER

Mr. Oscar Jerman
239 Riverside Road
Columbus, Ohio 43210

Mr. Thomas J. Weiss
Manager, Survey Division
Acme Engineering Company, Inc.
5868 Fanshawe Drive
Omaha, Nebraska 68131

Glossary of Grammatical Terms

Some of these terms are defined in the section where they figure prominently. But since many of these terms also occur in other sections where they are not defined, this glossary is provided for the convenience of the curious but puzzled reader.

active verb. See **passive verb.**

adjective clause. An adjective clause is a dependent clause that modifies a noun or a pronoun, much as a simple adjective does.

The relative pronouns **who, which,** and **that** often appear at the head of the adjective clause, serving as the connecting link between the modified noun or pronoun and the clause, which then follows.

The car, **which was old and battered,** served us well.

Those are the houses **that I love best.**

Sometimes the relative pronoun is unexpressed but understood:

The book **I was reading** held my attention. (Here **that** is understood: The book **that** I was reading.)

See **dependent clause, relative pronoun, restrictive adjective clause, nonrestrictive adjective clause, modifier.**

adverb clause. An adverb clause is a dependent clause that modifies a verb or verbal, much as a simple adverb does.

161

Glossary of Grammatical Terms

The subordinating conjunction (**when, because, so that,** etc.), which appears at the head of the clause, links the adverb clause to the word that it modifies.

When I was ready, I took the examination.

I took the examination **because I was ready.**

To take an examination **when you are not ready** is dangerous. (Here the adverb clause modifies the infinitive **to take.**)

See **dependent clause, subordinating conjunction, verbal, modifier.**

antecedent. An antecedent is the noun that a pronoun refers to or "stands for."

In the previous sentence, for example, the antecedent of the relative pronoun **that** is **noun.** In the sentence "The mother told her son that his check had arrived," **mother** is the antecedent of the pronoun **her,** and **son** is the antecedent of the pronoun his.

See **relative pronoun.**

auxiliary verbs. Auxiliary verbs are those function words—"helping" words (hence, "auxiliary")—that accompany other verb forms to indicate tense or mood or voice.

The following words in boldface are auxiliary verbs:

He **will** walk to work. He **is** walking to work. He **has** walked to work.

He **has been** walking to work. He **could** walk to work. He **must** walk to work.

He **was** driven to work.

See **function words, mood, voice.**

collective noun. A collective noun is a noun that designates a group or class of individuals—e.g. **committee, family, jury, army, faculty** (of a university), **team, crew.**

See **summary noun.**

comma splice. A comma splice is the use of a comma, instead of a coordinating conjunction or a semicolon, between the two independent clauses of a compound sentence.

He could not tolerate noise, noise made him nervous and irritable.

Since the comma is a separating device rather than a joining device, it must be accompanied in this sentence by a coordinating conjunction (here **for**), or it must be replaced with a semicolon.

See **independent clause, compound sentence,** and **coordinating conjunction.**

complement. A complement is the word or phrase, following a verb, that "completes" the predicate of a clause.

A complement may be (1) the object of a transitive verb (He hit **the ball**); (2) the noun or noun phrase following the verb **to be** (He is **an honors student**); or (3) the adjective following the verb **to be** or a linking verb (He is **happy.** The milk tastes **sour.**).

See **transitive verb, linking verb, to be, predicate complement,** and **noun phrase.**

complex sentence. A complex sentence is one that consists of one independent clause and one or more dependent clauses.

The following complex sentence has two dependent clauses—the first one an adverb clause, the second an adjective clause:

When he got to the microphone, he made a proposal **that won unanimous approval.**

As used by grammarians, the term has nothing to do with the length or complexity of the sentence.

See **independent clause** and **dependent clause.**

compound sentence. A compound sentence is one that consists of two or more independent clauses.

He was twenty-one, but she was only eighteen.

Young men are idealists; old men are realists.

See **independent clause** and **comma splice.**

compound word. A compound word is a combination of two or more words functioning as a single word.

There are compounds that function as a noun (a **stand-in**), as an adjective (**eighteenth-century** literature), as a verb (they **pistol-**

Glossary of Grammatical Terms

whipped him), or as an adverb (he had to comply **willy-nilly**). Some compounds have been used so often that they are written out with no space and no hyphen between the component parts (e.g. **handbook, postoffice**). Other compounds, especially those used as adjectives, are written with a hyphen (e.g. his **never-say-die** attitude). When in doubt about whether a compound should be hyphenated, consult a dictionary.

coordinate. Words, phrases, and clauses of the same grammatical kind or of equal rank are said to be "coordinate."

A pair or series of nouns, for instance, would be a coordinate unit. An infinitive phrase yoked with a participial phrase would not be a coordinate unit, because the phrases are not of the same grammatical kind. An independent clause would not be coordinate with a dependent or subordinate clause, because the two clauses are not of equal rank. An alternative term for **coordinate** is **parallel.**

See **parallelism** and **coordinating conjunction.**

coordinating conjunction. A coordinating conjunction is a word that joins words, phrases, or clauses of the same kind or rank. It joins nouns with nouns, verbs with verbs, prepositional phrases with prepositional phrases, independent clauses with independent clauses, adverb clauses with adverb clauses, etc.

A coordinating conjunction cannot be used to join a noun with an adjective, a prepositional phrase with a gerund phrase, or an independent clause with a dependent clause.

The coordinating conjunctions are **and, but, or, for, nor, yet, so.**

See **coordinate, correlative conjunctions,** and **subordinating conjunction.**

correlative conjunctions. Correlative conjunctions are coordinating conjunctions that operate in pairs to join coordinate structures in a sentence.

The common correlative conjunctions are **either . . . or, neither . . . nor, both . . . and, not only . . . but also,** and **whether . . . or.**

By this act, he renounced **both** his citizenship **and** his civil rights.

See **coordinate** and **coordinating conjunction**.

dangling verbal. A dangling verbal is a participle, gerund, or infinitive (or a phrase formed with one of these verbals) that is either unattached to a noun or pronoun or attached to the wrong noun or pronoun.

Raising his glass, a toast was proposed to the newlyweds by the bride's father.

In this sentence, the participial phrase **raising his glass** is attached to the wrong noun (**toast**) and therefore is said to be "dangling" (it was not the **toast** that was doing the **raising**). The participial phrase will be properly attached if the noun **father** is made the subject of the sentence:

Raising his glass, the bride's father proposed a toast to the newly-weds.

See **verbal** and **verbal phrase**.

demonstrative adjective. A demonstrative adjective is an adjective that "points to" its noun.

The singular forms are **this** (for closer objects—**this** book) and **that** (for more distant objects—**that** book); the plural forms are **these** and **those**.

dependent clause. A dependent clause is a group of words that has a subject and a finite verb but that is made part of, or dependent on, a larger structure by a relative pronoun (**who, which, that**) or by a subordinating conjunction (**when, if, because, although,** etc.).

There are three kinds of dependent clause: adjective clause, adverb clause, and noun clause.

A dependent clause cannot stand by itself; it must be joined to an independent clause to make it part of a complete sentence. A dependent clause written with an initial capital letter and with a period or question mark at the end of it is one of the structures that are called "sentence fragments." An alternative term is **subordinate clause**.

Glossary of Grammatical Terms

See **independent clause, finite verb, adjective clause, adverb clause, noun clause, subordinating conjunction.**

finite verb. A finite verb is a verb that is fixed or limited, by its form, in person, number, and tense.

In the sentence "The boy runs to school," the verb **runs** is fixed by its form in person (cf. **I run, you run**), in number (cf. **they run**), and in tense (cf. **he ran**). The verbals (participle, gerund, infinitive) are considered **infinite verbs** because although they are fixed by their form in regard to tense (present or past), they are not limited in person or number. The minimal units of a clause, whether it is dependent or independent, are a subject (a noun phrase) and a finite verb:

Bells ring. (but not: Bells ringing)

See **predicate verb, noun phrase, verbals.**

function words. Function words are those "little words" in the language that have very little vocabulary meaning but that perform such vital functions as connecting or relating other words in the sentence.

Sometimes called "particles," function words comprise all such words in the language as the following:

(1) articles or determiners (in front of nouns): **the, a, an, this, that, these, those, all, some,** etc.

(2) prepositions (for connecting or relating their objects to some other word in the sentence): **of, from, above, on, at,** etc.

(3) coordinating conjunctions (for joining words, phrases, and clauses of equal rank): **and, but, or, for, nor, yet, so.**

(4) subordinating conjunctions (for joining clauses of unequal rank): **when, if, although, because, that,** etc.

(5) auxiliary verbs (for indicating changes in tense and mood): **will, shall, have, may, can, would, should,** etc.

(6) conjunctive adverbs (for providing logical links between clauses): **however, nevertheless, moreover, therefore,** etc.

(7) **not** with **do** or **does** or **did** (for negating a verb):

He **does not** love his mother.
He **did not** love his mother.

fused sentence. A fused sentence is the joining of two or more independent clauses without any punctuation or coordinating conjunction between them.

He could not believe his eyes mangled bodies were strewn all over the highway.

A fused sentence is also called a **run-on sentence** or a **run-together sentence.**

See **independent clause** and **comma splice.**

genitive case. The genitive case, a term derived from Latin grammar, is the case formed in English by adding **'s** or **s'** to the ending of nouns and some pronouns (e.g. **someone's**) or by using the preposition **of** followed by a noun or pronoun.

The most common use of the genitive case is to indicate possession: the **boy's** book, the arm **of the boy.**

Some of the other uses of the genitive case are as follows:

genitive of origin: **Beethoven's** symphonies

subjective genitive: the **king's** murder (i.e. the murder that the king committed)

objective genitive: the **king's** murder, the murder **of the king** (i.e. the king as the victim of a murder)

genitive of composition: a ring **of gold**

partitive genitive: a piece **of cheese**

The personal pronouns form the genitive case by a special spelling: **his, her, its, your, our, their.**

The genitive formed by adding **'s** or **s'** to nouns is often called the **possessive case.**

gerund. A gerund is a word that is formed from a verb but that functions as a noun.

Because of its hybrid nature as part verb and part noun, a gerund may take an object, may be modified by an adverb, and may serve in the sentence in any function that a noun can perform.

167

Glossary of Grammatical Terms

Since, like the present participle, it is formed by adding **-ing** to the base verb, one can distinguish the gerund from the participle by noting whether it functions in the sentence as a noun rather than as an adjective. The following are examples of the gerund or gerund phrase performing various functions of the noun:

As subject of the sentence: **Hiking** is his favorite exercise.

As object of a verb: He favored **raising the funds by subscription.**

As complement of the verb **to be:** His most difficult task was **reading all the fine print.**

As object of preposition: After **reading the book,** he took the examination.

The latter sentence would be considered a dangling verbal if it were phrased as follows: After reading the book, the examination had to be taken.

See **verbal phrase** and **dangling verbal.**

independent clause. An independent clause is a group of words that has a subject and a finite verb and that is not made part of a larger structure by a relative pronoun or a subordinating conjunction.

The following group of words is an independent clause because it has a subject and a finite verb:

The **boys tossed** the ball.

The following group of words has the same subject and finite verb, but it is not an independent clause because it is made part of a larger structure by the subordinating conjunction **when:**

When the boys tossed the ball.

The **when** turns the clause into an adverb clause and thereby makes it part of a larger structure—a sentence consisting of a dependent clause (the adverb clause) and an independent clause (which must be supplied here to make a complete sentence).

See **dependent clause, finite verb, subordinating conjunction,** and **relative pronoun.**

Glossary of Grammatical Terms

infinitive. An infinitive is a word that is formed from a verb but that functions in the sentence as a noun or as an adjective or as an adverb.

Capable of functioning in these ways, the infinitive is more versatile than the participle, which functions only as an adjective, or the gerund, which functions only as a noun. The infinitive is formed by putting **to** in front of the base form of the verb.

Here are some examples of the infinitive or infinitive phrase in its various functions:

As noun (subject of sentence): **To err** is human; **to forgive** is divine.

As adjective (modifying a noun—in this case, **place**): He wanted a place **to store his furniture.**

As adverb (modifying a verb—in this case, **waved**): He waved a handkerchief **to gain her attention.**

The following infinitive phrase would be considered a dangling verbal:

To prevent infection, the finger should be thoroughly washed. (Corrected: To prevent infection, you should wash the finger thoroughly.)

See **verbal phrase** and **dangling verbal.**

inflection. The inflection of a word is the change of form that it undergoes to show grammatical relation in its context or to express modification of its meaning.

The inflection of the verb *to be* appears in the entry **to be** below.

intransitive verb. An intransitive verb is a verb that expresses action but that does not make an object.

Intransitive verbs cannot be turned into the passive voice. Most action verbs in English have both transitive and intransitive uses, like **I ran swiftly** (intransitive) and **I ran the streetcar** (transitive). But some verbs can be used only transitively, like the verb *to emit*, and some verbs can be used only intransitively, like the verb *to go*. If in doubt about whether a particular verb can be used both transitively and intransitively, consult a dictionary.

Glossary of Grammatical Terms

The following verbs are all used intransitively:

He **swam** effortlessly.

They **slept** for twelve hours.

She **quarreled** with her neighbors.

See **transitive verb, passive verb,** and **voice.**

juncture. Juncture is a grammatical feature only of the spoken language. It concerns the ways in which we divide and articulate the stream of sound to make it intelligible to native speakers of the language.

There is the kind of juncture that operates within and between words to help us discriminate between spoken phrases like "ice cream" and "I scream" or between "great rain" and "gray train." Another group of junctures makes use of various kinds of pauses or lengthening out of syllables to mark off the boundaries and terminations of utterances. This latter kind of juncture is roughly related to the punctuation system—commas, semicolons, periods, and question marks—of the written language.

linking verb. Linking verbs are those verbs of the senses like **feel, look, smell, taste, sound,** and a limited number of other verbs like **seem, remain, become, appear,** that "link" the subject of the sentence with a complement.

Linking verbs are followed by an adjective or a noun or a noun phrase:

The sweater **felt** soft. (adjective as complement)

He **appeared** calm. (adjective as complement)

He **remains** the president of the union (noun phrase as complement)

See **to be, complement, predicate complement,** and **noun phrase.**

modifier. A modifier is a word, phrase, or clause that limits, specifies, qualifies, or describes another word.

In the phrase "the red barn," the adjectival modifier **red** helps to specify or describe the particular barn being talked about. In the phrase "ran swiftly," the adverbial modifier **swiftly** describes the manner in which the action designated in the verb **ran** was done. Phrases and clauses also modify nouns and verbs:

the girl **with the flowery hat** (prepositional phrase modifying **girl**)

the barn **that is painted red** (adjective clause modifying **barn**)

he ran **down the street** (prepositional phrase modifying **ran**)

he ran **because he was frightened** (adverb clause modifying **ran**)

Besides modifying verbs, adverbs also modify adjectives and other adverbs:

It was an **unusually** brilliant color. (modifying the adjective **brilliant**)

He ran **very** swiftly. (modifying the adverb **swiftly**)

See **adjective clause, adverb clause,** and **squinting modifier.**

mood. Mood is that aspect of a verb which indicates the speaker's attitude toward the expressed action or condition. The **indicative mood** is used for statements of fact (The report **is** true); the **imperative mood** is used for commands (**Be** still!); the **subjunctive mood** is used to indicate hope or desire (I pray that they **be** happy), possibility (If it **be** true . . .), or condition (If he **were** here . . .). Except for the verb **to be,** the subjunctive forms of verbs are identical with the indicative forms except in the third-person singular of the present tense—e.g. **if he go** instead of **if he goes.**

nominative case. The nominative case is the form that a noun or pronoun must take when it appears as the subject of a clause or as the complement of a linking verb or of the verb **to be.**

In modern English, however, a writer has to be concerned about the nominative form only of some pronouns, because now nouns change their form only in the possessive case (**boy's, boys'**) and in the plural (**boy, boys; man, men**). The personal pronouns, however, and the relative pronoun **who** are still inflected (e.g. **he, his, him; who, whose, whom**). The nominative case of the relative pronoun **who** is **who.** The nominative case of the personal pronouns are as follows: **I, you, he, she, it, we, they.**

Glossary of Grammatical Terms

The wrong case (the objective or accusative case) of the pronoun is used in this sentence:

Me hate the smell of burning rubber.

See **complement** and **inflection.**

nonrestrictive adjective clause. A nonrestrictive adjective clause is an adjective clause that supplies information about the noun or pronoun that it modifies but information that is not needed to identify or specify the particular noun or pronoun being talked about.

My father, **who is a college graduate,** cannot get a job.

In this sentence, the adjective clause **who is a college graduate** supplies information about the father, but that information is not needed to identify which father is being talked about. The particular father being talked about is sufficiently identified by the **my.**

A nonrestrictive adjective clause must be separated with a comma from the noun or pronoun that it modifies.

See **adjective clause, restrictive adjective clause,** and **modifier.**

noun clause. A noun clause is a dependent clause that can serve almost every function that a noun or pronoun or noun phrase can serve: as subject of the sentence, as an appositive to a noun, as the complement for a verb, as object of a preposition, but not as an indirect object.

The subordinating conjunctions that most often introduce a noun clause are **that** and **whether**—although **that** is sometimes omitted when the noun clause serves as the object of a transitive verb.

That he would make the grade was evident to everyone. (subject of sentence)

He said **he would not come.** (object of verb; **that** is omitted here, but it is just as correct to say **that he would come**)

The fact **that I had been sick** did not influence their decision. (in apposition to **fact**)

They asked me about **whether I had seen him recently.** (object of the preposition **about**)

See **dependent clause, noun phrase,** and **complement.**

Glossary of Grammatical Terms

noun phrase. A noun phrase consists of a noun or a pronoun and all of its modifiers (if any).

In the following sentence all of the words in boldface would be considered part of the noun phrase, which is dominated by the noun **house:**

The big, rambling, clapboard house on the hill belongs to Mrs. Adams.

See **verb phrase** and **verbal phrase.**

parallelism. Parallelism is the grammatical principle that words, phrases, or clauses joined in a pair or in a series must be of the same kind.

Nouns must be coupled with nouns; prepositional phrases must be coupled with prepositional phrases; adjective clauses must be coupled with adjective clauses.

Parallelism breaks down, for instance, when a noun is yoked with an adjective or a prepositional phrase is yoked with a participial phrase. Parallelism has been preserved in the following sentence, because all the words in the series that serves as the predicate complement of the verb **was** are adjectives:

The engine was **compact, durable,** and **efficient.**

See **coordinate** and **coordinating conjunction.**

participle. A participle is a word that is formed from a verb but that functions as an adjective.

Because of its hybrid nature as part verb and part adjective, a participle may take an object, may be modified by an adverb, and may modify a noun or a pronoun.

Pulling his gun quickly from his holster, the sheriff fired a shot before the burglar could jump him.

In that sentence, the participle **pulling** takes an object (**gun**), is modified by the adverb **quickly** and by the prepositional phrase **from his holster,** and modifies the noun **sheriff.**

The **present participle** is formed by adding -**ing** to the base form of the verb: **pulling, jumping, being.**

The **past participle** is formed by adding -**ed** or -**en** to the base

Glossary of Grammatical Terms

form of the verb or by a special spelling: **pulled, beaten, left, bought.**

The **perfect participle** is formed with **having** plus the past participle form: **having pulled, having beaten, having left.**

The **passive participle** is formed with **having** plus **been** plus the past participle form: **having been pulled, having been beaten, having been left.**

See **verbal phrase** and **dangling verbal.**

passive verb. A passive verb is the form that a predicate verb takes when we want to indicate that the subject of the sentence is the receiver, not the doer, of the action.

The form that we use when we want to indicate that the subject is the doer of the action is called the **active verb.**

Only transitive verbs can be turned into the passive form. The passive verb is made by using some form of the verb **to be** (e.g. **am, is, are, was, were, has been**) and the past participle of the base verb.

The shepherds **tend** the sheep. (active verb)

The sheep **are tended** by the shepherds. (passive verb)

See **predicate verb, transitive verb, past participle, to be.**

possessive case. See **genitive case.**

predicate complement. Some grammarians use the term **predicate complement** to refer to any noun, pronoun, or adjective that follows or "completes" the verb, whether it be a transitive verb, a linking verb, or the verb **to be.** Other grammarians use the term **object** for the noun or pronoun that follows a transitive verb and reserve the term **predicate complement** for the noun, pronoun, or adjective that follows a linking verb or the verb **to be.**

He is the **president.** (noun following the verb **to be**)

She became the **breadwinner.** (noun following the linking verb)

The pie tastes **good.** (adjective following the linking verb)

See **complement, transitive verb, linking verb, to be.**

Glossary of Grammatical Terms

predicate verb. A predicate verb is the finite-verb part of the verb phrase that constitutes the whole predicate of a dependent or independent clause.

In the following sentence, the word in boldface is the predicate verb of the independent clause:

The man **guided** the dogsled through the blinding snowstorm.

See **finite verb** and **verb phrase.**

relative pronoun. The relative pronouns **who, which, that** serve a grammatical function in an adjective clause (as subject of the clause, as object or predicate complement of the verb of the clause, as object of a preposition in the clause) and also as the connecting link between the adjective clause and the noun or pronoun that the clause modifies.

Who is the only one of these relative pronouns that is inflected: **who** (nominative case), **whose** (possessive case), **whom** (objective case).

See **dependent clause, adjective clause,** and **antecedent.**

restrictive adjective clause. A restrictive adjective clause is an adjective clause that identifies or specifies the noun or pronoun that it modifies, that "restricts" the meaning to a particular person, place, thing, or idea.

Baseball players who are under contract to a duly franchised professional team are eligible for a pension.

In this sentence, the adjective clause **who are under contract to . . . team** specifies those baseball players who are eligible for a pension. If that adjective clause were enclosed with commas (that is, if it were a **nonrestrictive** clause), the sentence would mean that *all* baseball players are eligible *because* they are under contract to a professional team—a quite different meaning from the sentence that does not have commas enclosing the adjective clause.

A restrictive adjective clause should *not* be separated with a comma from the noun or pronoun that it modifies.

See **adjective clause, nonrestrictive clause,** and **modifier.**

Glossary of Grammatical Terms

run-on sentence. See **fused** sentence.

sentence fragment. See **independent clause, dependent clause,** and **finite verb.**

squinting modifier. A "squinting modifier" is a metaphorical way of referring to an adverb or an adverbial phrase that is placed between two words that it can modify. Because by position it "looks both ways," it results in an ambiguous sentence.

For example:

The candidate whom we favored **enthusiastically** praised our platform.

Since the adverb **enthusiastically** occupies a position between two verbs that it can modify (**favored** and **praised**), we cannot be sure whether it was the favoring or the praising that was done with enthusiasm. Shifting the adverb to a position before **favored** or after **platform** will relieve the ambiguity.

See **modifier.**

subordinating conjunction. A subordinating conjunction is a word that serves as the connecting link between an adverb clause or a noun clause and a word in some other structure.

The most common subordinating conjunctions that connect an adverb clause to the verb or verbal that the clause modifies are **when, whenever, because, since, although, though, while, as, after, before, unless, until, in order that, so that.**

The two subordinating conjunctions that serve as the link between the noun clause and another structure are **that** and **whether.** The conjunction **that** is often omitted when the noun clause functions as the object of a verb:

He said [that] the committee would not accept the proposal.

See **coordinating conjunction, adverb clause, noun clause.**

summary noun. A summary noun is a word that "sums up" an idea or set of particulars presented in the previous sentence. It is usually accompanied by one of the demonstrative adjectives **this, that, these, those.**

He answered telephones, stuffed envelopes, rang doorbells, collected money, and distributed literature. This **work** [or These **activities**] won him a secure position on the candidate's compaign staff.

To avoid the vagueness or ambiguity of reference that may result from beginning a sentence with only a **this** or a **these,** the writer should use a summary noun along with **this** or **these** (or **that, those**).

See **collective noun** and **demonstrative adjective.**

terminal punctuation. Terminal punctuation is the period or question mark placed after a string of words to signal the end of a sentence or utterance.

Commas, semicolons, and colons—sometimes called **internal punctuation**—are used to mark the boundaries of phrases and clauses within the sentence. An alternative term for **terminal punctuation** is **end punctuation.**

to be. To be is the infinitive form of the most frequently used verb in the English language, one that can be followed by a noun, a pronoun, an adjective, an adverb of place (e.g. **there, here, upstairs**), the preposition **like** plus the object of that preposition (e.g. He is **like his father**), a verbal or verbal phrase, or a noun clause.

Here are the various forms of **to be,** as it changes in number, person, and tense: **am, is, are, was, were, shall be, will be, has been, have been, had been, shall have been, will have been.**

Some form of **to be** along with the present participle of the base verb is also used to form the progressive tense of the English verb: He **was going** to the doctor regularly. He **had been going** to the doctor regularly.

Some form of **to be** along with the past participle of the base verb is also used to form a passive verb: He **was struck** on the head. He **has been struck** on the head.

See **linking verb, predicate complement, passive verb,** and **participle.**

Glossary of Grammatical Terms

transitive verb. A transitive verb is a verb expressing action that terminates in, or is received by, an object.

The object of a transitive verb can be a noun or noun phrase, a pronoun, a verbal or verbal phrase, or a noun clause.

They **destroyed** the village. (noun as object)

They **shot** him. (pronoun as object)

He **favors** giving me another chance. (gerund phrase as object)

He **will try** to break the lock. (infinitive phrase as object)

He **proposed** that everyone in the room be allowed to vote. (noun clause as object)

Only transitive verbs can be turned into a passive verb.

See **intransitive verb** and **passive verb.**

verb phrase. A verb phrase is a group of words consisting of a verb and all of its auxiliaries (if any), all of its complements (if any), and all of its modifiers (if any).

In the following sentence, all words in boldface would be considered part of the verb phrase (a structure dominated by the verb):

The army **has been severely restricted in its operations.**

See **noun phrase, verbal phrase, predicate verb, auxiliary verb, modifier.**

verbal. A verbal is the general name applied to participles, gerunds, and infinitives.

These words are called "verbals" because they are formed from verbs, but because they are not finite verbs, they cannot, by themselves, serve as the predicate verb of an independent clause or a dependent clause.

See **participle, gerund, infinitive, finite verb, predicate verb.**

verbal phrase. A verbal phrase is a group of words consisting of a participle or a gerund or an infinitive and all of its complements (if any) and all of its modifiers (if any).

In the following sentence, all words in boldface would be

considered part of the verbal phrase, which is dominated by the participle **leaving:**

Leaving behind all of its heavy equipment, the army pressed forward quickly.

voice. Voice is that aspect of a verb which shows the relation of the subject to the action, i.e. whether that of performer or recipient. The former is called **active voice** (I was loving), the latter **passive voice** (I was loved).

See **passive verb.**

Commonly Misspelled Words

accept (cf. except)
accidentally
acquire
acquaintance
address
all right
already (cf. all ready)
arithmetic
athletics

believe
benign
business

cemetery
changeable
chief
choose (cf. chose)
conscience
correspondent

definite

dependent
design
devise (cf. device)
diminution
disappearance
dispel

effect (cf. affect)
embarrass
environment
exaggerate
existence

familiar
fascinate
flagrant
forty (cf. fourth)
fragrant
friend
fulfill or fulfil
    (but not fullfill)

List of Commonly Misspelled Words

government

harass
height
hindrance

independent
irresistible
its (cf. it's)

judgment

library
literature
lose (cf. loose)

maintenance (cf. maintain)
mathematics
miniscule
miracle
miscellaneous
mischief

necessary
neighbor
noticeable
nuisance

occasion
occurrence
occurred
offered
omitted

parallel
peculiar

preceding (cf. proceeding)
preferred
prejudice
principal (cf. principle)
privilege

quite (cf. quiet)

receive
referring
relieve
remuneration
resemblance
reverence

seize
separate
similar
special
stationary (immobile)
stationery (writing materials)
succeed

than (cf. then)
their (cf. there)
threshold
too (cf. to)
tragedy
truly

usually

whose (cf. who's)
withhold

List of Commonly Misspelled Words

Add your own list of troublesome words:

1.
2.
3.
4.
5.
6.
7.
8.
9.
10.
11.
12.

Index

Index